"I have wrestled with the issue of assurance of salvation...not just as ...counseling timid souls but as a sinner trusting in God. What a great help is *Kept for Jesus*! Handling the relevant biblical texts with clarity and precision, Sam Storms has crafted real ministry with this book, working by the Spirit to plant the security of union with Christ in the believer's heart."

Jared C. Wilson, Pastor, Middletown Springs Community Church, Middletown Springs, Vermont; author, *Gospel Wakefulness* and *The Pastor's Justification*

"With care and compassion, Sam Storms engages in a wide-ranging discussion of the love of God, blasphemy against the Holy Spirit, spurious faith versus saving faith, human dignity and human depravity, the nature of eternal security, God's preserving power in faithful Christians, the problem of apostasy, and much more. Not shying away from the controversial nature of his topic and tackling head-on dozens of difficult passages, Storms offers an engaging book that deals biblically, theologically, and practically with the all-important matter of assurance of salvation."

Gregg R. Allison, Professor of Christian Theology, The Southern Baptist Theological Seminary

"Is your errant friend unsaved or simply backslidden? This book contains a great overview of what the Bible teaches about eternal security, the perseverance of the saints, God's sovereignty, and free will. Clear, readable, and compelling, this is a must for anyone who wants to understand the Reformed view on the assurance of salvation."

Mary A. Kassian, Professor of Women's Studies, The Southern Baptist Theological Seminary; author, *Girls Gone Wise in a World Gone Wild*

"Too often the gospel is reduced to only wiping away sin's debt. Storms shows us a more wonderful gospel of love and direct relationship with God in which Christ is inseparable from us, keeping us, and holding us as family. Storms is a pastor of pastors, walking us through the thorny issues—such as the warning passages—and into green pastures of communion with our Savior. He calls us into the beautiful tension and transformation of God's forever grace."

Daniel Montgomery, Pastor, Sojourn Community Church, Louisville, Kentucky; Founder, Sojourn Network; author, *Faithmapping* and *Proof*

"Do you worry that you will lose your salvation? Do you feel confident in God's love for you? This book will help you feel secure in God's promises over you. Jesus said of his people: "I give them eternal life, and they will never perish, and no one will snatch them out of my hand" (John 10:28). Sam Storms once again demonstrates his pastoral wisdom as he lovingly lays the foundation for eternal security."

Adrian Warnock, author, *Hope Reborn* and *Raised with Christ*

"This is classic Sam Storms: warm, thoughtful, clear, and wise. Not all readers will agree on every detail, but all will be well served by working through the issues with such an insightful guide. Throughout the book, God's protection of his people shines through—and so do the joy and security that this brings to all who trust him."

Andrew Wilson, Pastor, Kings Church Eastbourne, East Sussex; author, *If God, Then What?* and *Unbreakable*

"Sam Storms has given us a book that is fair, humble, straightforward, and helpful. He consistently presents views that oppose his own and frequently admits he does not have all the answers. He argues biblically and passionately for the truth that God keeps true believers saved to the end and focuses on the Christian life and rejects errant views, including those that cut the biblical cord between God's keeping us and our keeping on in faith, love, and holiness. This is a good book, and I am happy to recommend it."

Robert A. Peterson, Professor of Systematic Theology, Covenant Theological Seminary

KEPT FOR JESUS

Other Crossway books by Sam Storms

Chosen For Life: The Case for Divine Election, 2007

The Hope of Glory: 100 Daily Meditations on Colossians, 2008

More Precious Than Gold: 50 Daily Meditations on the Psalms, 2009

Signs of the Spirit: An Interpretation of Jonathan Edwards's "Religious Affections," 2007

A Sincere and Pure Devotion to Christ: 100 Daily Meditations on 2 Corinthians 1–6, 2010

A Sincere and Pure Devotion to Christ: 100 Daily Meditations on 2 Corinthians 7–13, 2010

To the One Who Conquers: 50 Daily Meditations on the Seven Letters of Revelation 2–3, 2008

Tough Topics: Biblical Answers to 25 Challenging Questions, 2013

KEPT
· FOR ·
JESUS

WHAT THE NEW TESTAMENT REALLY TEACHES ABOUT ASSURANCE OF SALVATION AND ETERNAL SECURITY

SAM STORMS

CROSSWAY

WHEATON, ILLINOIS

Kept for Jesus: What the New Testament Really Teaches about Assurance of Salvation and Eternal Security

Copyright © 2015 by Sam Storms

Published by Crossway
1300 Crescent Street
Wheaton, Illinois 60187

Cover design: Jesse Owen, 10AM Design

First printing 2015

Printed in the United States of America

Trade paperback ISBN: 978-1-4335-4202-2
ePub ISBN: 978-1-4335-4205-3
PDF ISBN: 978-1-4335-4203-9
Mobipocket ISBN: 978-1-4335-4204-6

Library of Congress Cataloging-in-Publication Data
Storms, C. Samuel, 1951–
    Kept for Jesus : what the New Testament really teaches
about assurance of salvation and eternal security / Sam
Storms.
        pages cm
    Includes bibliographical references and index.
    ISBN 978-1-4335-4202-2 (tp)
    1. Assurance (Theology)—Biblical teaching. 2. Bible. New
Testament—Theology. I. Title.
BS680.A86S76   2015
234—dc23   2014034075

Crossway is a publishing ministry of Good News Publishers.

VP   25 24 23 22 21 20 19 18 17 16 15
15 14 13 12 11 10 9 8 7 6 5 4 3 2 1

To the elders and pastors at Bridgeway Church
with deep gratitude for your friendship,
your prayers of support, and especially
your faithfulness to the gospel

Contents

INTRODUCTION

Meet Charley. On second thought, you probably already know him—or someone whose life bears a striking resemblance. Perhaps Charlene would be a more suitable name for some of you. In any case, his (her?) life will pose for us a painful and difficult dilemma. Let me explain.

Charley was born into a Christian family. His parents were devout followers of Jesus, and both of his siblings, an older brother and a younger sister, came to faith in Christ and remained vibrant and deeply committed to him throughout their lives.

Charley was raised in the church and was usually present whenever the doors were open, whether at a Sunday service, a youth meeting, special events throughout the week, or a summer retreat. When he turned twelve, he professed faith in Jesus, largely through the influence of his parents and older brother. He was baptized soon thereafter and was discipled by his youth pastor over the course of the next few years. Charley's faith appeared to be quite vibrant and joyful. He endured the same trials and temptations as do virtually all teenaged boys, but he never wandered far or failed to repent when he sinned. He prayed every day and read his Bible and was growing in his understanding of God.

Following graduation from high school, he fell in with a different group of friends at college. They challenged his faith and insisted that he was being naïve to believe in Jesus. The arguments they regularly threw in his face were fairly typical:

Only ignorant and uneducated people believe that Jesus was really born of a virgin and rose physically from the dead.

Evolution is a proven scientific fact and makes the existence of God unnecessary.

If there is really an all-powerful and good God in charge of the universe, why is there so much evil and injustice?

If you keep this "faith" that you obviously inherited from your parents, you'll never be able to drink and sleep around and experience the really fun stuff in life.

It wasn't long before Charley stopped attending church and eventually declared himself to be an atheist. He grew increasingly angry at the institutional church and nurtured a deep resentment toward those who influenced him while growing up, having become convinced that they hid the truth from him and only wanted to control his life.

Charley is now thirty, already twice divorced, an alcoholic, and painfully bitter and unpleasant to be around. He wants nothing ever again to do with Christianity.

So what's up with Charley? What happened? Without getting too technical, it's important that you understand how Christians from various traditions and denominations explain this.

The majority of those who identify with the Nazarene, Methodist, Assembly of God, Church of Christ, and Free-Will Baptist traditions, among others, insist that Charley was, in all likelihood, genuinely born again at the age of twelve. He truly trusted Christ and was truly saved. He was justified or declared righteous in the sight of God. He became an adopted son of God and was forgiven all his sins. The Holy Spirit came to indwell Charley and to empower him for godly living. But through a variety of factors and for a whole host of reasons, Charley willfully repudiated everything he once affirmed, denied his faith, and *apostatized*. Notwithstanding all that friends, family, and even God himself could do to persuade him to stay true to Christ, he walked away in denial of the Lord he once embraced. Charley forfeited his salvation. He is now, at the age of thirty, a child of the Devil and headed for eternal condemnation, cut off from Christ.

Although no one really likes to be labeled, we will call people who embrace this view "Arminians," named after the late sixteenth- and early seventeenth-century Dutch theologian James Arminius. Be it noted, however, that not all Arminians deny the eternal security of the believer.[1] More on this later.

There is another view that some of you have never encountered. People who embrace it come from a wide variety of backgrounds, including some Southern Baptists, dispensationalists, and others from so-called independent Bible churches. They insist that once Charley was truly saved, he was forever saved. Even though he walked away from faith and repudiated Jesus, he is still safely secure in the arms of his heavenly Father and will, *regardless of how he lives and dies*, end up in heaven for eternity. Charley *ought* to have walked in obedience and faithfulness, and we *should* encourage him to do so. But he doesn't have to. If he chooses to live a life in unbelief and immorality, he is still saved.

However, whereas he doesn't lose his salvation, his denial of Jesus and his sinful behavior will lead to the loss of rewards in heaven. He gains entrance into the eternal kingdom of God, but he will not experience the joy of knowing his heavenly Father's approval, and he will suffer the loss of rewards that other, more faithful Christians, will receive.

While not affiliated with any particular denomination or tradition, that view has come to be known by many of its critics as "anti-

---

[1] Arminius himself wrote, "I never taught that a *true believer can either totally or finally fall away from the faith, and perish;* yet I will not conceal, that there are passages of Scripture which seem to me to wear this aspect." *The Writings of James Arminius*, vol. 1 (Grand Rapids, MI: Baker, 1977), 254 (emphasis original). Arminian scholar Roger E. Olson concludes that "Arminius himself never settled the matter." *Arminian Theology: Myths and Realities* (Downers Grove, IL: InterVarsity, 2006), 187.

nomianism." Now, please understand, those who advocate this view would never call themselves "antinomians." The term *antinomian* comes from two Greek words that together mean "against the law." It has often been used to describe those who say that although you ought to obey the principles and moral laws of the Scriptures, you won't lose your salvation if you don't. You'll only lose your reward. In other words, you *should* persevere in holiness of life, but if you don't, you're still a child of God.

Those whom I'm calling "antinomians" argue that if you are once saved, you are always saved, regardless of how you live or what you believe after you initially come to saving faith in Jesus.

Finally, those who typically come from Presbyterian as well as Southern Baptist and other traditions associated with what is known as "Calvinism" or the "Reformed" faith (because of their close association with the Protestant Reformation and its leaders Martin Luther and John Calvin) look at Charley and draw one of two conclusions.

First, some conclude that if Charley was truly saved at the age of twelve, he is still saved at the age of thirty, and will, by God's grace and the convicting work of the Holy Spirit, eventually come to his spiritual senses and return to the Lord. This may come only after enduring severe discipline from his heavenly Father, but eventually God will bring him back. In some cases, people like Charley are disciplined straightway into heaven; that is to say, the discipline of the Lord results in their physical death. They die prematurely under the discipline of God, but they are saved eternally.

Second, others conclude that the likely explanation for Charley's departure from his professed faith in Christ is that he was never genuinely born again. His so-called faith was spurious. His apparent life of obedience was prompted by factors other than a genuine love for Jesus. He was self-deluded and deceived everyone who knew him. If he had been truly born again, he would have persevered in his faith.

As you can see, the Arminian says that Charley was truly saved, apostatized from the faith, and is now lost. The antinomian says that Charley was truly saved, is still truly saved, but will suffer the loss of rewards in the age to come because of his disobedient lifestyle. The Calvinist says Charley may have been truly saved, and if so, he will come under the discipline of the Lord, who will either restore him to his walk with Jesus or take him home to heaven prematurely. Alternatively, says the Calvinist, Charley was never truly saved, and his failure to persevere in a life of obedience is evidence that his profession of faith was just that, a verbal profession, and not the genuine faith that possesses forgiveness of sins.

As you will quickly see, I hold to the Calvinist or Reformed view. I agree with the Arminian when he says that perseverance in faith and holiness is necessary for final salvation, but I disagree with him when he says that a born-again person can fully and finally apostatize from the faith, thereby losing his salvation. Likewise, I agree with the antinomian that all those truly born again are eternally secure in their salvation, but I disagree when he says that a born-again person can live in unrepentant sin throughout the course of his life, be encouraged with the assurance of salvation, and expect to find himself in heaven.

I will strive to be as objective as I can in explaining what others believe, but there is no escaping the fact that I am solidly, energetically, and passionately committed to the view that when a man or woman is born again by the Spirit of God and justified by faith in Jesus Christ alone, he or she will persevere in faith unto life's end, even though that perseverance may be a bit bumpy and inconsistent along the way. That person, however, will never utterly abandon Christ because the Father has promised never to utterly abandon us but to keep us safe and secure through faith.

WHY DO PEOPLE REJECT THE DOCTRINE OF ETERNAL SECURITY?

Many of you live with deep-seated anxiety about eternity, an anxiety that occasionally degenerates into outright fear. "Am I *really* saved?

I *think* I'm saved. I *hope* I'm saved. But these doubts are driving me insane. What if I sin again today, just like I did yesterday and the day before that? Will I eventually cross the point of no return? Will God, at some point, cease to love me and just give up on me?"

Some of you live confidently in the assurance of your salvation. You're even happy and joyful about it. Others who aren't saved are persuaded they are. Their so-called assurance is little more than presumption and arrogance. Then, of course, some are convinced that although they are saved today, that may change. What are we to make of this, and what does the Bible say about it?

As a Calvinist who believes in the eternal security of God's elect, I often ask, Why do people disagree and embrace the Arminian view? Why do people doubt or deny the doctrine of eternal security? Why do so many insist that they've known friends or family members who once were genuinely born again but through some sin or backslidden rebellion have lost their salvation? There are several reasons for these beliefs.

Often the culprit is *tradition*: "That's what I was raised to believe. I can't bring myself to believe that Mom and Dad and the preacher and all my friends were wrong." This is a far more powerful influence, subtle and unconscious though it be, than most of us realize. I'm not immune to it any more than you are. To be open to another view seems like we are saying, "The past was all for naught. It meant nothing." To some it feels as if they must question the integrity or value of people and pastors whom they love and respect and who've been a powerful influence in their lives. That is difficult for many to cope with.

Undoubtedly a major contributing factor is the presence in the New Testament of several so-called problem passages. Two such texts are found in Hebrews 6 and 2 Peter 2, both of which I attempt to explain later in the book. Let's be honest: every view has problem passages! There are biblical texts that seem to run counter to each of the three views I presented. We have to deal honestly and fairly with

them and ask, Which view does the best job of accounting f(
thing the Bible says on this topic? That being said, many are.   ...i-
ians simply because they believe that's what the Bible teaches.

I also think many fear that if people are told they can't lose their
salvation, they will indulge in gross immorality. They fear it will lead
people to think: "If I can't lose my salvation, I'll do whatever I please"
(see Rom. 6:1–4). In other words, the legitimate concern for holiness
leads some to an illegitimate rejection of security.

As noted, others have known people like Charley (or Charlene),
whom they are convinced are Christians, who later give every indication of having fallen away. Believing them to have truly been born
again, the only explanation is that they have lost their salvation.

Part of the blame can also be laid at the feet of certain religious
leaders who need people to be insecure in their salvation in order
to retain control over them. They cultivate anxiety and doubt in the
hearts of people in order to exert greater control over their lives
(and often their money). Fear is a powerful means by which to keep
people under one's religious thumb.

Many believe that eternal security diminishes a person's moral
responsibility. It places too much emphasis on God's sovereignty
and not enough on human free will.

Finally, for some, the exhortations and warnings in Scripture to
be holy, to persevere, and to endure make sense only if the possibility exists that one may choose not to do so.

So my aim in the pages ahead is twofold. First, I want to convince
you who embrace either the Arminian or antinomian view that you
are mistaken in your belief. I make no apologies for that. Second,
I want to deepen everyone's confidence in the supremacy of God's
saving and preserving grace. I want you to conclude each chapter
more joyful and grateful than when you started reading, because
you know that your sins are forgiven and that God will never, ever
leave you or forsake you.

1

How Deep the Father's Love for Us

Among the many things we say about God, nothing is more foundational than the declaration "God is love." Nothing else in Christianity makes sense apart from the belief that God is love. God's love explains everything, whether it be the incarnation of Christ, his sinless life, his atoning death, his resurrection, and his return to earth, not to mention the very existence of heaven and eternal life.

Why is it, then, that so many Christians struggle to believe it? Why is it that our boldest and loudest assertion concerning God is often embraced and believed with the least degree of confidence? Why is it that simultaneous with our public declarations of God's love, there is a lingering, private doubt concerning its reality? We don't typically have problems with the other divine attributes. I rarely hear Christians express anxiety over the notion that God is truth or that he is holy or that he is just and omnipresent and all-powerful. But it's another matter entirely when his love is mentioned.

Let me be clear about this. I'm not saying that Christians deny that God is love. Rather, it's that they often doubt, in the depths of their soul, that he loves them individually, that his love for them is the sort that endures despite their many sins and failures. The anxiety that grips their hearts is borne of a fear that one day God will quite simply count his losses and cut them loose. After all, isn't that what happens in so many human relationships, whether in marriage or between what we thought were lifelong friends? So how can I be sure God's love isn't cut from the same cloth? How can I know that the love he has shown sinners in the death of his Son, Jesus Christ, isn't suspended upon how well I perform in the aftermath? How can I be assured that God won't turn out like so many others who once pledged their love for me only to bail out at the first sign of trouble?

The answers to those questions are addressed in a variety of ways in this book, based on a variety of biblical texts. But nowhere are they more explicitly set forth than in the words of Jesus himself in the Gospel of John. It's the perfect place to begin our exploration of eternal security.

JOHN 6

We are going to look at two passages in John's Gospel. In the first, John 6:37–44, Jesus tells us explicitly that the will of the Father is that he "should lose nothing of all that he has given me, but raise it up on the last day. For this is the will of my Father, that everyone who looks on the Son and believes in him should have eternal life, and I will raise him up on the last day" (John 6:39–40).

Jesus's argument in these verses must be carefully noted. On several occasions in John's Gospel, divine election is described in terms of God the Father *giving* certain persons to God the Son (6:37, 39; 10:29; 17:1–2, 6, 9, 24). In each of these cases the giving of men to Christ precedes and is the cause of their receiving eternal life. Those who are given to the Son include not only the present company of disciples who believe in Jesus but also the elect of future ages who will come to faith through the gospel. Jesus looks upon them as already his (John 17:20–21; see also John 10:16; Acts 18:10), even though they have not yet believed in his name. They are his because they were given to him by the Father in eternity past.

Of special importance to us is what Jesus says about how those whom the Father has given to him come to him and whether those who come can ever lose their salvation. It will prove helpful to look at this in terms of three impossibilities.[1]

First, Jesus says it is morally and spiritually *impossible* for a person to come to Christ apart from the "drawing" of that person by God the Father (6:44, 65).

Second, Jesus says it is *impossible* for someone whom the Father draws *not* to come to him. He says in verse 37, "All that the Father gives me *will* come to me." In other words, just as it is impossible for people to come to Christ apart from the Father drawing them, so also is it impossible for people *not* to come to Christ if the Father *does* draw them.

To these two impossibilities Jesus adds a third: he says that when people do come through the drawing of the Father, it is *impossible* for them to be cast out. Look again at verse 37: "And whoever comes to me I will never cast out." The point is that those whom the Father gives to the Son, who therefore come to the Son, will be received by the Son and shall never perish. The verb translated "cast out" in verse 37 is used several times in John (2:15; 6:37; 9:34–35; 10:4; 12:31) and always means to cast out someone or something already in. Thus the emphasis here is not so much on receiving the one who comes (although that is true enough in itself) but on preserving him or her.

Who would suggest that Jesus Christ would refuse to accept what his Father has given him? If the Father was pleased to make a gift of certain sinners to his most blessed Son, you may rest assured that the Son will neither despise nor deny his Father's gracious generosity. The certainty of ultimate and absolute salvation for those who come to the Son is reaffirmed in verses 38–40. Their life in Christ is eternal and irrevocable because that is the will of the Father, a will or a purpose that the whole of Christ's person and work was designed to secure and that shall ultimately be fulfilled (Pss. 115:3; 135:6; Dan. 4:34–35; Eph. 1:11; Acts 4:28).

---

[1] Some of what follows has been adapted from my book *Chosen for Life: The Case for Divine Election* (Wheaton, IL: Crossway, 2007). Used by permission of Crossway.

So what did Jesus come to do? He came to do the Father's will (v. 38). What is the Father's will? The Father's will is that all those he has given to the Son be fully and finally saved (v. 39).

Before we leave John 6, it's important to understand that searching and studying Scripture is not simply a matter of asking, "What is it saying?" but also, "Is what it's saying compatible with what *we're* saying?" Let me explain.

To deny eternal security means the possibility exists that some who come to the Son will in fact be cast out. It means the possibility exists that the will of the Father and of the Son that all born-again believers be raised up on the last day will not, in fact, be fulfilled. It means that although Jesus is determined to ensure that every born-again Christian is fully and finally saved, the possibility exists that every born-again Christian might be fully and finally damned for eternity. Are you prepared to say that?

To deny eternal security means that when Jesus said he *will* raise up finally and forever all those given to him by the Father, he was misleading us. He should have said, "I *hope* to do so," or "I'll *give it my best shot*," but the fact remains that he *won't* raise up all those given to him by the Father. Some of them, based on the Arminian view, will have apostatized.

How can Jesus say he will raise up all the Father gives him if in fact he will not, because some who truly believe in him finally and forever fall away and forfeit eternal life?

JOHN 10

Now look with me at Jesus's words concerning his sheep in John 10:

> My sheep hear my voice, and I know them, and they follow me. I give them eternal life, and they will never perish, and no one will snatch them out of my hand. My Father, who has given them to me, is greater than all, and no one is able to snatch them out of the Father's hand. I and the Father are one. (John 10:27–30)

Jesus grounds his confidence in the safety of his sheep in the incomparable omnipotence of his Father. It is because there is no one greater or more powerful than God the Father that the sheep are secure. Was Jesus mistaken in his assessment of the Father's power and purpose?

What will you do with his declaration that his sheep "will *never* perish" (John 10:28)? A more literal translation is, "They shall not, by no means, ever perish." This is an absolute, unassailable negative. Would Jesus have said this if in fact *many* of his sheep *will* perish? If so much as one true child of God can ever perish, Jesus has deceived us.

"And no one will snatch them out of my hand" (v. 28). Not the attacking wolf (v. 12), or the thieves and robbers (vv. 1, 8), or anyone.

Can we agree on one thing before going further? Will you concur that "no one" means *no one*? You don't have to go to seminary or be able to read Greek to figure that out. "My Father, who has given them to me, is greater than all, and no one is able to snatch them out of the Father's hand." God the Father himself stands behind God the Son in keeping the sheep in the fold. Jesus holds us tightly. God holds us tightly. Who can steal from God? Who has the strength or the cunning or the power to outwit and outmuscle almighty God?

In verse 28 Jesus says, "No one will snatch them," whereas in verse 29 he says, "No one *is able* to snatch them." Some may attempt to snatch them, but they cannot succeed because the Son and the Father are united in purpose and power to keep them secure.

Some may reply, "Okay, perhaps no one *else* can snatch me from God's hand. But what if *I myself* through my sin and selfishness and stupidity wriggle free and jump out of my own accord?"

Is your power of choice greater than God's? Is your will more powerful than his? Look again at Jesus's words: "No one" is all inclusive. If eternal security is false, then Jesus is saying, "No one can snatch them out of my Father's hand; oh, that is, except for every one of the sheep." But if you mean *everyone*, you don't say *no one*.

"No one" is the opposite of "everyone." Jesus doesn't say, "No one except for the person himself." In Romans 8:38–39 all creatures are excluded as a threat to loss of salvation. In John 10 the Creator himself is excluded as well.

Ask yourself this question: If Jesus wanted to teach eternal security, how could he have done it better or more explicitly than the way he does it here? If you yourself wanted to assert eternal security, how could you do it better than by using the words of Jesus in John 10? Someone might object, "They won't perish so long as they remain sheep." But the text doesn't say that, does it? The assertion of the text is precisely that sheep always remain sheep. The point of the text is: "Once a sheep, always a sheep."

If Jesus wanted us to believe that some of his sheep could cease being sheep and suffer eternal death, why did he say his sheep will never suffer eternal death and no one can snatch them from him or from his Father? Surely Jesus is not guilty of the crassest form of double-talk. In other words, "They will never perish" = "They shall always stay sheep."

Another might ask, "But what if some sin I commit or a failure in life or a weakness or a lapse of faith occurs repeatedly?" How much sin does it take to lose one's salvation? What does a good shepherd do with wandering sheep? He wouldn't be a good shepherd if he didn't restore them when they wander. Our security is ultimately dependent on God's character and commitment, not on ours. People say, "If we change, we lose our salvation." No. We can't lose it, not because we can't change, but because God can't.

In the final analysis, the only reason I affirm the perseverance of the saints is that I believe in their preservation by the Savior. We persevere only because he preserves us in faith. Praise be to God!

CONCLUSION

Now, how might we think of Charley, and what should we say to him?

First, I would never say to him what the antinomian would: "Hey,

Charley. You really shouldn't be living this way. You are missing out on tremendous blessings. Please return to the Lord and his church. But if you don't, if you remain unrepentant in your sin, you will still spend eternity with me and all other Christians in heaven. After all, you made a decision for Christ and that's all that matters. Once saved, always saved, even though you will lose out on those spiritual rewards that you otherwise might have received. As grieved as I am by your lifestyle choices, I rejoice in knowing that you are my brother in Christ now and forever, even if you refuse to acknowledge that it is true."

No! Never, ever, give assurance of salvation to someone who is persisting in unrepentant sin, regardless of how allegedly sincere they were when they allegedly believed in Christ. I may not have the right to tell Charley that he isn't saved. After all, only God knows our hearts. But I certainly will never give him the assurance that he is.

Second, I would never say to him what the Arminian would: "Hey, Charley. I'm brokenhearted over the fact that you have turned your back on your Savior and have forfeited the blessings of the new birth, adoption, and justification. Turn from your sin, repent, and you can receive forgiveness and be saved yet again from your sins."

The simple fact is that I don't know whether Charley was ever truly born again. I don't know with complete certainty if his professed faith in Christ was authentic and life giving. Only God knows. What I do know is this: if Charley is among those whom the Father gave to the Son, if he truly came to Christ in faith and embraced him as Lord and Savior, Jesus will never, ever cast him out. Jesus *will* raise him up on the last day in fulfillment of the Father's will. No one will ever snatch Charley out of the loving hands of the Father and the Son.

But if Charley persists in unrepentant sin and hard-hearted unbelief, he will by his lack of perseverance demonstrate that in all likelihood, he never knew Jesus, and Jesus never knew him. On that basis you can rest assured that I will never give him a false assurance of salvation simply because he claims once to have genuinely trusted Christ. As Jesus said, "You will recognize them by their fruits" (Matt. 7:20).

In any and every case, I will pray for Charley (or Charlene), as I hope you will.

2

So Close yet So Very Far Away

We have been looking at a young man named Charley, who professed faith in Christ at the age of twelve and appeared to live a Christian life for quite a few years, only to walk away from Christianity while in college and end up in angry atheism and bitterness toward both the faith in which he had been raised and the Christian church. I asked how we might explain Charley's experience.

Was he truly born again at the age of twelve and later apostatized from the faith, thereby losing or forfeiting his salvation? That's the answer of Arminian theology and those in the Nazarene, Methodist, Assembly of God, Church of Christ, and Free-Will Baptist traditions.

Others argue that Charley was truly saved at twelve and still is now at the age of thirty, even though he lives in open, defiant, unrepentant sin and unbelief, and even though he may continue to live this way until his death. He didn't lose his salvation but will likely suffer the loss of rewards in the coming kingdom. Those who believe this we are calling "antinomians."

The view that I believe is most consistent with Scripture is that if Charley was genuinely born again at age twelve, he still is, and God will bring discipline to his life and eventually restore to him the joy of his salvation. In some cases, as was true with Ananias and Sapphira in Acts 5 and some of the Christians in Corinth in the first century, this discipline of the Lord leads to premature physical death. But the child of God remains a child of God.

A more likely scenario is that, notwithstanding his profession of faith at twelve, Charley never genuinely repented and trusted Christ. His religious or spiritual experience may have had a temporary impact on his life, sufficient to deceive not only him but also others into thinking he was truly saved. But had he truly been born again, he would have persevered in faith and obedience. Whatever rebellion or backsliding he may have experienced, God would eventually have brought conviction of sin to his heart, repentance to his life, and restoration of his relationship with Christ.

In this chapter we are going to examine three well-known passages in Matthew's Gospel, each of which will help us in its own way come to a deeper understanding of the nature of true, saving faith and its counterfeit.

MATTHEW 7:15–23

What do you do when people claim to be Christian, attend church on a regular basis, know the definitions of all those big theological words, and are even dedicated to ministry and appear to be successful, not simply in the little things but especially in the supernatural dimension? Jesus warns us not to be gullible or to believe everything they say or that we see. This is clearly his point in our first passage, Matthew 7:15–23.

False prophets are nothing new. God warned the people through Jeremiah in the sixth century BC. "An appalling and horrible thing has happened in the land," declared the Lord; "the prophets prophesy falsely, and the priests rule at their direction; [and] my people love to have it so" (5:30–31a). Again in 14:14 we read: "The LORD said to me: 'The prophets are prophesying lies in my name. I did not send them, nor did I command them or speak to them. They are prophesying to you a lying vision, worthless divination, and the deceit of their own minds.'"

The New Testament describes on several occasions the threat posed by false prophets in the church (see Acts 20:29–31; 2 Cor. 11:13–15; 2 Pet. 2:1–3; Jude 4). Look at how Jesus describes them.

He speaks first of their deception. They "come to you in sheep's clothing, but inwardly are ravenous wolves" (Matt. 7:15). I'm not worried about the openly heretical lie or the false teacher who makes no bones about the fact that he is teaching heresy. Jesus here has in mind those who sneak in secretly, bearing all the regalia of religiosity: robes and academic degrees and theological vocabulary and persuasive speech and a charismatic personality. They sound orthodox. They appear to say and do all the right things, so far as we can see. But inwardly they are "ravenous wolves" who desire to consume you personally, financially, and spiritually.

Eventually, though, their fruit will betray them. The imagery Jesus uses in verses 16–19 would have meant more to his original audience than to us. In Palestine there is a certain thornbush called the buckthorn with small, black berries that from a distance closely resemble grapes. And there is a certain thistle with a flower that from a distance can be mistaken for a fig. The point is there may be a superficial resemblance between the true and the false, but on closer inspection you see that a buckthorn cannot yield grapes, nor can a thistle produce figs. Given enough time, people will always be true to their nature. The rotten tree will eventually produce rotten fruit.[1]

Concerning the false teachers, the "fruit" Jesus has in mind is both their doctrine and their deeds, both what they teach and how they live. Sometimes it's more what they don't say than what they do. They scrupulously avoid difficult and demanding biblical truths such as God's holiness and human sinfulness and judgment and repentance and eternal punishment. Their preaching is intentionally vague and psychologically soothing.

"You will recognize them by their fruits" (v. 20). Jesus's point

---

[1] See D. A. Carson, *Matthew*, Expositor's Bible Commentary (Grand Rapids, MI: Zondervan, 1984), 191.

here is crucial. Eventually, given enough time, those who truly know God will display the fruit of the Spirit, whereas those who do not will produce rotten apples and worm-eaten oranges and toxic tomatoes. The conduct of one's life will invariably, over time, reveal the character of one's heart. This is why Jesus warns us of this ominous and unsettling truth: "Not everyone who says to me, 'Lord, Lord,' will enter the kingdom of heaven" (v. 21). Several things here deserve our close attention.

First, Jesus does not mean that we can dispense with professions of faith, as if what we say or declare is useless (see Rom. 9:9–10). Nor are we being told that addressing Jesus as "Lord" is wrong. Neither is Jesus saying that good works justify us in God's sight or earn entrance into the kingdom. As we'll see later on, we are not saved *by* good works, but we *are* saved *for* them.

Second, these whom Jesus has in mind are fervent and zealous. They are not ashamed of the name of Christ but shout aloud: "Lord! Lord!" They appeal to the fact that all their "works" are done in his name.

Third, they are probably convinced they are really saved. They will be astonished at the judgment seat on the final day. Their assurance of salvation is grounded solely in their profession, not their practice. Yes, they have works to which they may point, but not the kind or the quality that qualify as "the Father's will." What is the "will" of the Father? Later in John's Gospel Jesus says, "This is the work of God, that you believe in him whom he has sent" (John 6:29). And what are the "works" that bear witness to the reality of this faith? Just think back to the Beatitudes, earlier in the Sermon on the Mount. Poverty of spirit, humility, mourning for sin, purity of heart, hunger and thirst for righteousness, mercy, self-sacrifice, and love.

Fourth, how did these people come to be so deceived? One can't be certain, but they likely got swept up in the euphoria of supernatural displays of power and mysterious religious experiences and thought that such are the same as true spirituality and genuine love for God. So long as they could produce spectacular results and keep people in awe of their authority and spiritual prowess, less sensational things such as humility and love and prayer and repentance were ignored.

But if these are unbelievers, how can they perform miracles? Neither Jesus nor Matthew provides us with an answer, but it may be that they do so with God's permission, as was the case with Balaam in the Old Testament and Judas Iscariot in the New Testament. Both were unbelievers yet prophesied. Judas also apparently healed the sick and cast out demons. Theologians refer to such ability as the workings of "common grace." The grace and enabling power of the Holy Spirit can work in unbelievers, empowering them to do countless things that are beneficial, even though they remain unregenerate and lost in sin. People often lose sight of how much the Holy Spirit accomplishes for and through non-Christians, short of salvation itself. Conversely, of course, their claims may be spurious. The miracles they *claim* to have performed may be false.

The declaration in Matthew 7:23 is startling. Jesus says in effect, "I don't care about your miracles if you have no mercy. I don't care about your works of power if there is no purity. I don't care about your exorcisms if there is no encouragement. I have never known you in a saving way. You are strangers to me. All your activity, all your religious deeds that you thought were righteous and would earn your acceptance with my Father, are in fact lawless and loathsome. Depart from me!"

It would be possible to extend our Lord's comments to something like this: "Lord, Lord, were we not members of a church? Did we not support it with our finances? Did we not serve in children's ministry once a month, perhaps even twice a month? Lord, were we not good American citizens who paid our taxes?"

The primary point, as we consider this text, is that merely claiming to know Jesus and doing good and even supernatural deeds in the name of Jesus does not of itself mean that Jesus knows you. And

thus when such people are exposed or walk away of their own accord, we must not conclude that they were once truly saved but have
apostatized and lost their salvation.

Matthew 12:22–32[2]

It's not uncommon for people to say that someone they know who
was truly born again and trusted Christ for the forgiveness of his
sins has committed the "unpardonable sin" or has committed "blasphemy of the Holy Spirit" and is now lost and destined for eternal
death. I've encountered numerous Christians who were convinced
that they themselves had committed this sin. They typically point
to Matthew 12 to prove their position.

Make no mistake: knowing and resting in the truth that one's
sins are forgiven is an incomparable blessing and delight. This is
why the words of Jesus here in Matthew 12 are so unsettling:

> Therefore I tell you, every sin and blasphemy will be forgiven
> people, but the blasphemy against the Spirit will not be for-
> given. And whoever speaks a word against the Son of Man will
> be forgiven, but whoever speaks against the Holy Spirit will not
> be forgiven, either in this age or in the age to come. (vv. 31–32)

Are you confused by this? On the one hand, as we saw in a previous chapter, Jesus says in John 6 that whoever comes to him he will
by no means ever cast out. On the other hand, here in Matthew 12 he
says that whoever blasphemes the Holy Spirit will *never* be forgiven,
neither now nor in the age to come. Both statements must be true.
What, then, do they mean? Jesus's ominous declaration doesn't
occur in a vacuum. Something happened to provoke it. So let's look
at the context.

The religious leaders had just witnessed Jesus casting out a
demon from someone, and they concluded that Jesus did so because

[2] Much of what follows has been adapted from chap. 6 of my book *Tough Topics: Biblical Answers to 25 Challenging Questions* (Wheaton, IL: Crossway, 2013). Used by permission of Crossway.

he himself was possessed by Beelzebul or Satan. We are told that a man who was both blind and mute was brought to Jesus. Jesus proceeded to cast out the demon and heal the man. Instantly he could see and speak. The miracle was incontestable. No one doubted that he was truly blind and mute. And the scribes didn't doubt that he was also demonized. Matthew says that "all the people were amazed" (v. 23); they were astounded, knocked back on their heels. They were left breathless. This was an unusually overwhelming miracle. It was so undeniably supernatural that the people began to wonder whether Jesus might in fact be the Son of David, the Messiah.

Their options were limited. There were only two possible explanations for what happened. This was no magical sleight of hand—a case of some slick magician pulling a rabbit out of a hat or doing amazing things with a deck of cards. This man had been blind and mute, and everyone knew it. We've all heard stories of a perfectly healthy woman sitting in a wheelchair as if paralyzed, only to be "miraculously healed" by some unscrupulous charlatan who then quickly makes an appeal for money. But in the case of this young man, his healing was the work either of God or of the Devil. Since they refused to acknowledge that it was God, they had no other choice but to conclude Jesus did it by the power of Satan himself.

Our Lord's response was profound. In essence he said, "Satan may be evil, but he's not stupid!" That is to say, any kingdom or house or city that develops internal strife will ultimately self-destruct. Satan's domain is no different. Aside from God himself, Satan is probably the most intelligent being in the universe. He is not so insane as to permit internal division or civil war among his demons. Satan is committed to self-preservation. He will do nothing that might threaten or reduce his power. In other words, Satan would never be guilty of spiritual suicide. Jesus wasn't saying that there is harmony or trust or loyalty in Satan's kingdom. Undoubtedly every demon in existence is selfish and perverted. But Satan would never allow any demon to undermine his efforts. Quite simply, Satan does not cast out Satan.

This leads Jesus to declare that whereas all sins can be forgiven, even blasphemy against him (vv. 31–32a), "whoever speaks against the Holy Spirit will not be forgiven, either in this age or in the age to come" (v. 32).

I'll return to this in just a moment, but before I try to explain what the unforgivable or unpardonable sin is, I need to explain what it is not, because I assure you that some reading this are convinced they've committed it.

People have often said that the unforgivable sin is murder. If you kill an innocent human being, God will never forgive you. But consider Moses, David, and Paul, each of whom could easily have been charged with homicide.

Others have argued that adultery is the unforgivable sin. But, again, David committed adultery, yet it was he who wrote the majority of the psalms we sing and celebrate. And what about the woman taken in adultery in John 8 whom Jesus forgave and told to go and sin no more? And what about the Samaritan woman at the well in John 4?

Maybe the unpardonable sin is denying Jesus under pressure or threat of persecution. But consider Peter, who denied Jesus three times. Some have argued that suicide is the unforgivable sin. But no text in either the Old or New Testaments ever says any such thing.

There are probably quite a few of you who have lived in fear that you committed the unforgivable sin when you took the Lord's name in vain. Perhaps in a moment of rage or bitterness or disappointment you cursed the Lord or strung together a barrage of expletives or used the f-word repeatedly or some such thing. Or perhaps in your frustration and confusion you angrily declared that God doesn't exist or that he has miserably failed you. As serious as these sins are, they are not beyond forgiveness!

What Is the Unforgivable or Unpardonable Sin?

Jesus is specific in identifying the nature of this sin: it is blasphemy against the Holy Spirit. The religious leaders were not accused of blaspheming Jesus himself, a sin for which there is forgiveness (Matt. 12:32). Their sin was against the Holy Spirit because it was by the power of the Spirit that Jesus performed his healings and miracles. Jesus himself said in verse 28 that it was "by the Spirit of God" that he "cast out demons." Here we see that the life Jesus lived, he lived in the power of the Spirit. The miracles he performed, he performed in the power of the Spirit.[3]

The religious leaders were saying, "Jesus, we don't deny that a great healing miracle has occurred. We don't deny that you cast out a demon from that man. But the power by which you did it was Satan's."

Thus their sin was attributing to the Devil what the Spirit had done. They didn't deny the existence of the supernatural. They didn't deny the reality of the miracle. They simply said, in a remarkable display of hardness of heart and spiritual blindness, that the Devil had enabled him to do it.

But we still don't know why Jesus regarded this as so heinous a sin that it was beyond forgiveness. The answer is found in the relationship between Jesus and the religious leaders and how they responded to him. Their repudiation of Jesus was not the result of ignorance or lack of evidence or because they believed the negative report of someone else who didn't like Jesus. Blasphemy of the Holy Spirit is willful, wide-eyed, persistent, unrepentant slandering of the work of the Spirit, attributing to the Devil what is undeniably divine. These people had seen as clearly as anyone could see and understood as lucidly as anyone could understand that Jesus performed his miracles by the power of the Spirit. Yet they defiantly

---

[3] For a recent and excellent defense of this truth, see Bruce Ware, *The Man Christ Jesus: Theological Reflections on the Humanity of Christ* (Wheaton, IL: Crossway, 2012).

insisted, contrary to what they knew to be true, that it was Satan who empowered him.

The miracles Jesus performed were credentials of heaven. The religious leaders declared them to be the credentials of hell. They didn't merely deny Jesus's deity. They, in effect, declared him to be a demon. His family may have thought he was mentally deranged, but the Pharisees declared him to be morally demonic.

Theirs was not a one-time, momentary slip or an inadvertent mistake in judgment. This was a persistent, lifelong rebellion in the face of inescapable and undeniable truth. Blasphemy of the Holy Spirit is not a careless act committed only once in a moment of rage or rebellion but a calloused attitude over time, a persistent defiance that hardens the heart.[4]

The Pharisees had been present when Jesus healed the sick. They saw him perform miracles up close and personal. They witnessed him raising the dead. They watched with their very eyes as skin infected with leprosy suddenly and decisively became clean and smooth and whole. They heard him teach with power and authority. They watched as demons fled his presence as he set free those in bondage. They watched with their eyes as he gave sight to the blind. Notwithstanding all this, they openly and persistently and angrily and arrogantly declared that he did it all by the power of the Devil.

Blasphemy of the Holy Spirit, therefore, is not just unbelief, the sort of unbelief or rejection or doubt that is so typical in our world. It is defiance of what one knows beyond any shadow of doubt to be true. It is not mere denial but determined denial; not mere rejection but wanton, willful, wicked, wide-eyed rejection.

This sin, therefore, is unforgivable not because there is a defect in the atoning death of Jesus. It is unforgivable not because there is a limit to God's grace and mercy or because of some other shortcoming in the character of God.

---

[4] See the excellent treatment of this problem passage in Carson, *Matthew*, 290–92.

The New Testament makes plain that sins are forgiven only if people repent (cf. Mark 1:4, 14, 15; 4:12; 6:12; Acts 2:38; 5:31). They must turn from sin to God and trust his grace and follow him. So when Jesus says that "every sin and blasphemy will be forgiven people" (Matt. 12:31), he means every sin and blasphemy *from which you genuinely repent.*

Why, then, does Jesus seem to exclude one sin and one blasphemy from this promise—the blasphemy against the Holy Spirit? I think the reason is *that blasphemy against the Holy Spirit puts you beyond repentance, and therefore beyond forgiveness.*

John Piper has wisely pointed out that Matthew 12:32 is not an exception to verse 31.[5] Jesus is *not* saying, "All *blasphemies you repent of* will be forgiven except blasphemy against the Spirit." No. He is saying, "All blasphemies you repent of will be forgiven; but blasphemy against the Holy Spirit will not be forgiven because, by its very definition and nature, it makes it impossible for you any longer to repent." If a sin makes repentance impossible, then it is an unforgivable sin, because forgiveness is promised only to those sins from which we genuinely repent.

A sin from which one may repent is not the unpardonable sin. Therefore, those who are most worried that they may have committed the unpardonable sin have not. An unforgivable sin is one for which there is no concern, no conviction, no anxiety, and thus no repentance. Such a sin is so hard-hearted and willful and persistent and defiant that the one committing it couldn't care less that he or she is committing it.

Remember, Jesus was addressing unbelievers. He was describing first-century religious leaders whose hard-hearted hatred of him was so deep that they attributed the Spirit's work through him to Satan. So, yes, it is possible for people to put themselves beyond the possibility of forgiveness. But that is not God's fault. It is not for

[5] See his sermon on Mark 3:20–35, April 1, 1984, "Beyond Forgiveness: Blasphemy against the Spirit," http://www.desiringgod.org.

lack of mercy in him. It is not because he is limited in compassion or power or grace. It is because some who have seen, heard, and even tasted the truth have chosen to harden their hearts to the point that they have rendered themselves impervious to repentance and conviction.

Let me speak to those of you who are convinced you have committed the unforgivable sin or at least are fearful that you may have. A particular sin in your life may have caused you massive internal anguish. The guilt is piercing and relentless. The shame is so heavy and paralyzing that you feel as if every breath of spiritual life is being squeezed out of you.

Trust me, I know about this, because dozens and dozens of you have come to talk to me over the years. I can't begin to count the number who are broken and shaking and weep endlessly and lose sleep, and when they do sleep, they experience horrid nightmares because they are convinced they have committed a sin that God cannot or will not forgive.

If I've just described you, I tell you on the authority of God's Word—I tell you with absolute confidence and joy—you have not committed the unforgivable sin.

- People who are ashamed of their sin have not committed the unforgivable sin. The unforgivable sin is committed *shamelessly* over time.

- People who feel the conviction of the Holy Spirit in their hearts, who sense the piercing presence of guilt for having violated God's Word, have not committed the unforgivable sin. People who commit this sin feel no guilt. If anything, they are *proud* of what they've done.

- People who are in fear that they have committed the unforgivable sin have not. The heart given to this depth of depravity has *no fear of God or fear of judgment*.

- People who are *broken* and grieved by their sin have not committed the unforgivable sin.

The bottom line is that I know with a high degree of confidence when people have not committed the unforgivable sin. But I don't know when, if at all, people have committed a sin in such a way that they have put themselves beyond the forgiveness of God.

The unpardonable sin, therefore, or blasphemy of the Holy Spirit, is not a single sin committed by a Christian that results in the loss of salvation. It is a deep-seated, entrenched, lifelong disdain for Jesus that unbelievers, like the Pharisees of the first century, commit. People guilty of this sin remain unrepentant and defiant. Because this hard-hearted repudiation of Jesus is lifelong and puts one beyond the power of repentance, it is beyond the possibility of forgiveness.

Allow me for a moment to speak to the two sorts of people who most need to hear these two texts. Some of you have a conscience like concrete. You aren't in the least bothered by your sin or broken by your arrogance and presumption. You are spiritually hard-hearted and proud. You think you're saved. You point to your religious life, your church attendance, your faithfulness in tithing, your voting record, and the fact that you openly declare your allegiance to Jesus. To you Jesus says: "I don't know you. I never have." It's not that Jesus will confess his ignorance of your existence. He simply means, "You have no relationship with me. You never repented of your religion and cried out to me for forgiveness and devoted yourself by the grace of the Spirit to live in a way that pleases my Father. Depart from me."

It is possible for such unregenerate people to put themselves beyond the possibility of repentance and thus beyond the hope of forgiveness, so I appeal to you: repent, believe the gospel, and embrace Jesus alone as Lord.

There is another sort of conscience at the other end of the spiritual spectrum, so to speak. I'm talking about the hyperactive, excessively tender conscience. This is the person suffocating in shame and burdened by guilt and wallowing in self-contempt. This is the man who lives in constant, daily, hourly fear that he's committed the unforgivable sin, perhaps multiple times. Far from walking in confidence and the assurance of salvation, he lives in hopelessness and in the paralyzing fear that God has forever forsaken him. I assure you, he has not.

Jesus speaks to both kinds of conscience today. Hear him.

Matthew 13:1–9, 18–23

What we've seen so far is that it is possible for people to hear God's Word, profess faith in Jesus, perform supernatural deeds in ministry, and yet be eternally lost. It isn't because they are saved and later apostatize. It is because their so-called faith is shallow and spurious. Nowhere is this possibility more vividly seen than in the famous parable of the sower.

The point of this parable is that the kingdom of God is coming into the world just like seed sown by a farmer. In spite of Satan's opposition and the hardness of human hearts, the kingdom is gradually bearing fruit among God's chosen. The kingdom is here now, yielding fruit, but the final harvest is yet to come. Contrary to the expectations of the Jews, the kingdom displays only moderate success, much as the farmer's seed only partially takes root and yields a crop. The kingdom does not force itself upon people; it must be willingly received.

Thus the kingdom is both present and future. It is present, bearing its fruit, even as the seed sown by the farmer yields its fruit. It is also future, to be revealed and consummated in glory, even as the full harvest of the farmer's crop is yet to come. But is there any other significance in the details of the parable? Yes, but only because Jesus himself interprets them for us.

The sower = Christ (or anyone who proclaims the word of the gospel)
The seed = the word of the kingdom / the gospel
The soils = the hearts of men and women
The birds = satanic/demonic opposition
Thorns = worry and deceit of world and wealth

Those who've studied this parable closely point out that it isn't important that there were four soils; there could as easily have been three or seven. We can't conclude from the fact that only one of four produced fruit that Christians will always be a minority in the world. The meaning wouldn't change if the reason for the failure of the seed was different: rodents could have eaten the seed instead of birds; an unseasonable cloudburst could have washed it away instead of it being scorched by the sun; tender shoots of grain could have been crushed underfoot instead of being choked by thorns.[6]

Clearly, though, Jesus wants us to consider what kind of soil our hearts prove to be. He is issuing a challenge concerning how we hear the word of the gospel and respond to it. There are here four kinds of people, four kinds of response to the gospel of the kingdom.

First (v. 19), there is the man or woman who may hear and listen yet understands nothing. The human heart can be so pounded and beaten down by the traffic of sin that it is like spiritual concrete, impervious to the gospel. Before long, Satan has come and taken the seed away. No matter how effectively or long or short you or I may preach, this person is unaffected.

Second (vv. 20–21), there is the impulsive person who converts at a revival meeting, a retreat, or a youth camp. Wherever emotions are high and the gospel is portrayed as promising health, wealth, ease, and popularity, people will believe. This is epidemic today. The response is enthusiastic but shallow; there is no deep consideration of the gospel and its implications; there is no counting of the cost.

---

[6] Carson, *Matthew*, 304–14. Carson's exposition is especially insightful.

The response is quick and euphoric but false; it soon fades. Beware of so-called conversions that are all smiles and no repentance, much religious bravado but no brokenness over sin and no humility.

There is no root in that kind of belief. External pressures, trials, troubles, persecution, and expectations that aren't fulfilled soon bring this person back to reality. Like the sun beating down on a rootless plant, the shallowness of the soil is manifest. Notice that they "immediately" receive it with joy (v. 20), they endure "for a while," and then "immediately" fall away (v. 21). The time in between may be years. Many spend years in church until something doesn't go their way or life turns sour. They expect God to deliver them from every trial, and when he doesn't, they abandon their profession of faith. The gospel that they thought was the key to prosperity and popularity has now brought hardship, trial, and persecution.

Third (v. 22), there are those who profess faith in Jesus so long as it is convenient, comfortable, and fulfilling. They experience a momentary fervor that is soon replaced by thirst for more money and concern for reputation. Fashion, career, and prestige are like weeds that will ultimately choke off any hope of spiritual life. Being a follower of Jesus is okay so long as there's enough time for it. But if it should get in the way of a few more days at the lake or a couple more rounds of golf or illicit sex or whatever else it is that they consider so indispensable to life, well, so much the worse for following Jesus.

Fourth (v. 23), there are those who hear and receive the word and invest their lives in it; they not only embrace it as intellectually credible but also as spiritually satisfying. They are invested in the truth of Christianity such that they sacrifice everything to build upon it and entrust their lives to it, both now and for eternity. The proof of their conversion is their perseverance in bearing fruit.

Like the soils before them, they experience tribulation and persecution. They have cares and concerns in this world. They face the daily deceitfulness of riches and wealth. They are tempted to abandon the faith to gain more stuff and to advance their careers. They know what it's like to suffer loss for the sake of their relationship to Jesus. They struggle with a desire for other things. They don't always resist temptation successfully. Their faith falters on occasion. They have their doubts. But at no time do they abandon their confidence in Christ. At no time do they walk away from the hope of the gospel for the sake of money or fame or safety.

CONCLUSION

These three passages in Matthew's Gospel are a bit disconcerting, not because they undermine the truth of eternal security, but in the way they remind us how easy it is for some to be deceived about their relationship to God. Merely hearing the gospel avails little. Neither witnessing nor personally benefiting from the working of miracles testifies to the presence of saving faith. That initial emotional euphoria upon responding to the good news of the kingdom can quickly dissipate and die. That we all likely know men and women who heard and received and later ministered on behalf of the gospel, only later to have fallen away, is a sobering reality that ought to give us pause. But at no time should it lead us to conclude that those genuinely born of the Spirit can falter so as to finally fail to enter the kingdom of God. Such is the love of God for his own that he will never permit them to suffer eternal loss.

3

THE DANGERS OF FICKLE FAITH

Jesus himself said twice in the span of five verses that people are recognized by their fruits (see Matt. 7:16, 20). It is impossible to over-emphasize the importance of this principle. Jesus's point is simply that the essence of what you are on the inside will inevitably become evident on the outside. Or, to say it in different terms, *who* you are will eventually show in *how* you live.

As we saw in the previous chapter, Jesus used an illustration from a familiar feature in horticulture, known to everyone in first-century Palestine. "Every healthy tree bears good fruit, but the dis-eased tree bears bad fruit" (Matt. 7:17). Early on and from a distance you may not be able to differentiate among trees. They may look much the same. But eventually, over time, the fruit they bear will testify to the kind and quality of tree they are. If the tree is rotten and diseased, such will be the fruit it produces. If, on the other hand, it is alive and healthy, so too will be the fruit that comes forth.

The simple but profound truth that Jesus taught in Matthew 7:16–20 is that Christians produce moral and spiritual fruit that bears witness to the reality of what is on the inside. In the absence of such fruit, we should be extremely cautious about telling people that they are born-again children of God. We should be rightly sus-picious about their claim to conversion. If their behavior doesn't measure up to their beliefs, something's terribly wrong.

Some people have mistakenly thought that focusing on behavior puts too much emphasis on good works. To them, it sounds as if we are saying that good works are the condition for salvation or that good works are the basis for our acceptance with God. I assure you, I am saying no such thing. I do believe good works are essential but as the evidence of saving faith. Good works are not the root of our salvation but its fruit, which is to say, good works are not the cause of salvation but its consequence.

Perhaps the best way to say it is with a phrase made popular by both John Calvin and Martin Luther during the time of the Protestant Reformation: *Sola fides iustificat, sed non fides quae est sola*, or, in English, "Faith alone justifies, but not the faith that is alone." The faith that truly saves, that genuinely unites us to Christ, is a particular kind of faith. It is living, fruit-giving faith that invariably leads to personal holiness, good works, and a gradually transformed life. That is why Jesus and the authors of the New Testament so often say that if you want to know whether someone's claim to faith is real, test and taste the fruit.

Here in chapter 3 we are going to put this principle to the test by looking at a difficult but important passage in John's Gospel.

JOHN 15:1–6

In John 15:1–6 we read that God, as the vinedresser, lovingly "prunes" believers (v. 2). He cleanses, purges, and purifies them of whatever does not contribute to their spiritual maturity (or fruitfulness). This might occur in any number of ways, whether by discipline, teaching, or testing. The debate centers on what God does with the fruitless branches and what the latter represent. There have generally been three views of this passage.

The standard Arminian interpretation is that the fruitless branches are genuine Christians who, because of their fruitlessness, or because of their failure to persevere in holiness of life, lose their salvation. When Jesus says these branches will be "thrown into the fire, and burned" (v. 6b), he is referring to eternal punishment in hell.

Another perspective is that the fruitless branches are genuine Christians who, because of their fruitlessness, undergo divine discipline. Their removal and judgment is physical death, not spiritual death. They remain saved but are prematurely taken to heaven as a disciplinary response to their failure to walk in obedience to Jesus.

The other option for those who believe in eternal security is to understand the fruitless branches to be so-called disciples who experience only an external, superficial connection with Jesus. Although they believe and follow Jesus in one sense, their outward allegiance and verbal commitment to him is not the expression of having trusted Jesus sincerely for salvation. The fruitless branches, therefore, are not saved and never were.

I believe the third option is most consistent with what we read in the Gospel of John and in the rest of the New Testament. My reasons (six of them) for adopting this view and rejecting the others are as follows.

First, the implausibility of the Arminian view is seen in that Jesus declared in John 10:28–29 that those to whom he gives eternal life shall never perish. More decisive still is the word used in John 15:6. There Jesus says that the fruitless branches will be "thrown away" (a form of the Greek verb *ballo*, "to cast," "to throw," together with the adverb *exo*, "outside" or "out"). But in John 6:37 Jesus uses virtually identical terminology and says, "All that the Father gives me will come to me, and whoever comes to me I will never cast out" (*ekballo* with *exo*). The Arminian view would require that what Jesus *denied* could happen to a believer in 6:37, he affirms *will* happen in 15:6. In other words, Jesus says in 6:37 he will never cast out those who believe in him, but in 15:6 he says he will. Surely neither our Lord in speaking nor John in recording his words is guilty of the most obvious of theological contradictions.

Second, a weakness in the view that Jesus's words pertain to

believers under discipline is that what Jesus says of the destiny of
the fruitless branches reads more like eternal condemnation than
temporal chastisement. The fruitless branch is taken away (v. 2). The
fruitless branch is "thrown into the fire" and "burned" (v. 6; cf. Matt.
3:12; 5:22; 18:8–9; 25:41; 2 Thess. 1:7–8; Rev. 20:15).

Now, I suppose someone could make the case that this is the language or imagery that one would expect in describing what is done
with old, dead, fruitless branches. What else would one do with
them but burn them? So perhaps we shouldn't make too much of
it. Furthermore, in 1 Corinthians 3:15 Paul is speaking of Christians
when he says: "If anyone's work is burned up, he will suffer loss,
though he himself will be saved, but only as through fire." So this
second view isn't entirely implausible.

Third, the view that the fruitless branches are unregenerate is
supported by what John's Gospel says about unsaved believers. Although this sounds strange, John often portrays people as "believing" in Jesus who are clearly not born again. He clearly envisions
a stage in the progress of belief in Jesus that falls short of genuine
saving faith and thus falls short of salvation. A clear example is
found in John 2:23–24. There we read that "when he [Jesus] was in
Jerusalem at the Passover Feast, many believed in his name when
they saw the signs that he was doing. But Jesus on his part did not
entrust himself to them, because he knew all people." Here we see
that not all so-called belief is genuine, Spirit-wrought, saving faith.
People can in some sense believe in Jesus and never truly know him
as Lord and Savior. In that case, people were fascinated by the miracles Jesus performed. They believed "when they saw the signs that
he was doing." Their so-called belief or faith was grounded in their
surprise and infatuation with the supernatural. But clearly it was
not saving faith. It was not a belief that trusted and treasured Jesus
as Lord and Savior.

The point here is that people claim and actually do, in a sense,
believe in Jesus for any number of reasons other than a legitimate

desire to receive the forgiveness of sins and eternal life that he offers. Some believe (like these in John 2) because they are swept
away by the sensationalism and excitement of supernatural activity. Some believe because by identifying with the local church they
find instant friendships and social activities and a place to belong.
Some believe because they are looking for a way to soothe their
guilty conscience or to experience personal affirmation, or because
they long for transcendent meaning in their lives, and religion appears to provide it. Some believe because of pressure from family
or friends to conform. Some believe because they find Christianity
intellectually satisfying. I could go on citing reasons people believe
that have little or nothing to do with genuine, heartfelt repentance
and love for Christ and a passion to follow him.

Yet another instance is found in John 6. You may recall that after
Jesus insisted that those who follow him must eat his flesh and drink
his blood (v. 53), many were befuddled and bothered. We read in
verse 60 that "when many of his disciples heard it, they said, 'This
is a hard saying; who can listen to it?'" This is followed in verse 66
with the declaration, "After this many of his disciples turned back
and no longer walked with him." D. A. Carson explains:

> "Disciples" must be distinguished from "the Twelve" (cf.
> vv. 66–67). More importantly, just as there is faith and faith
> (2:23–25), so are there disciples and disciples. At the most el-
> ementary level, a disciple is someone who is at that point fol-
> lowing Jesus, either literally by joining the group that pursued
> him from place to place, or metaphorically in regarding him
> as the authoritative teacher. Such a "disciple" is not necessar-
> ily a "Christian," someone who has savingly trusted Jesus and
> sworn allegiance to him, given by the Father to the Son, drawn
> by the Father and born again by the Spirit. Jesus will make it
> clear in due course that only those who *continue* in his word

are *truly* his "disciples" (8:31). The "disciples" described here do not remain in his word.[1]

Yet another example is found in John 8 where John refers to certain Jews who had "believed" in Jesus (v. 31). Yet according to the verses that follow, these people are in fact slaves to sin (v. 34), indifferent to Jesus's word (v. 37), and children of the Devil (v. 44). They accuse Jesus of being demonized (v. 48); they are liars (v. 55) and guilty of mob tactics, including attempted murder of the one they have professed to believe (v. 59). They are said to have believed but are clearly not only unsaved but among the enemies of Jesus.

It is clear that in John's Gospel not all so-called belief or faith is authentic, Spirit-wrought, saving faith. What Jesus describes here can only be called "fickle faith," a degree of commitment, perhaps a willingness to agree with the truth of some of what Jesus said and a desire to follow him temporarily. There is also the possibility that these people had been swept up in the excitement of the crowd and captivated by the spiritual energy that surrounded Jesus. He was a magnetic personality, and many were inclined to follow him as much out of religious curiosity as out of genuine love. Clearly this applied to those Jewish people.[2]

To put it in as simple terms as I know how, one can in some sense believe in Jesus and declare oneself to be his disciple without ever having been saved in the first place. There is in John's Gospel, therefore, a transitory, superficial, surface faith or belief based solely on miracles witnessed but not grounded in or backed up by the fruit of a saving understanding of and trust in who Jesus really is. Such people are in some sense connected or united to Jesus, perhaps mentally or emotionally, such that they may even be called "disciples," yet they are not Christian disciples. These, I believe, are the unfruitful branches of John 15:2, 6.

---

[1] D. A. Carson, *The Gospel according to John* (Grand Rapids, MI: Eerdmans, 1991), 300.

[2] Although we can't be sure, this may also be the case in John 7:31 and 12:11, 37.

So how does one differentiate between genuine faith and fickle, false faith? Jesus tells us in John 8:31 that the mark of true faith is abiding or remaining in Jesus's word. To remain or abide in Jesus's word, says Carson, means that a person "obeys it, seeks to understand it better, and finds it more precious, more controlling, precisely when other forces flatly oppose it. It is the one who continues in the teaching who has both the Father and the Son (2 John 9; cf. Heb. 3:14; Rev. 2:26)."[3]

Abiding in Jesus does not make you a Christian. What makes you a Christian is the new birth and the saving faith that is its fruit. Abiding is not the condition for becoming a child of God. Abiding is the consequence or the evidence or the fruit of being a disciple of Jesus. You become a Christian by faith, the evidence of which is that you abide or remain in your devotion and pursuit of Jesus and in your desire to learn from him and love him.

Genuine, saving faith is the sort that not only learns what he says but also loves it. Genuine faith displays its true character by producing in the heart of the individual a persevering attachment to Jesus. Momentary, flash-in-the-pan commitment to Christ means nothing. We've all seen people who are excited today and out the exit tomorrow, men and women who display an attraction to religion and the benefits it can bring them, but who, during the routine experiences of daily life, are rarely heard to utter a distinctly Christian word or make a self-effacing sacrifice for the benefit of another or commit a distinctly Christian act. They are, in essence, indistinguishable from the world. Discipleship is not a sudden, short-lived enthusiasm about Jesus but a lifelong love affair, a lifelong dedication characterized by love and obedience.

Notice how Jesus describes those who supposedly believe in him: "You seek to kill me because my word finds no place in you" (John 8:37b). Christ's word does not operate in their lives, is given no

---

[3] Carson, *The Gospel according to John*, 348.

value in their thinking, has no role in their daily decision making, and gives no shape or direction to how they relate to God or others.

Listen carefully. These Jewish people were religious, law-abiding, monotheists. They believed in God. They faithfully attended their synagogue services. They committed no scandalous sins. In some sense of the word, they even believed in Jesus. Yet they had Satan for their father (v. 44).

We have an interesting example of this in Acts 8. A man named Simon, a magician, heard Philip preach the gospel and believed and was baptized (Acts 8:13). Well, then, you would think that settles it. He is definitely a child of God. He must be born again. Not exactly.

We read later in the story that when Simon saw the power of the Holy Spirit come upon the people of Samaria, he said: "Give me this power also, so that anyone on whom I lay my hands may receive the Holy Spirit" (8:19). Here is the apostle Peter's response:

> Peter said to him, "May your silver perish with you, because you thought you could obtain the gift of God with money! You have neither part nor lot in this matter, for your heart is not right before God. Repent, therefore, of this wickedness of yours, and pray to the Lord that, if possible, the intent of your heart may be forgiven you. For I see that you are in the gall of bitterness and in the bond of iniquity." And Simon answered, "Pray for me to the Lord, that nothing of what you have said may come upon me." (Acts 8:20–24)

Was Simon ever really saved? Some say yes. He truly believed and was even baptized and then apostatized and fell from grace and lost his salvation. But it seems clear to me that Simon's so-called belief was the same as those who believed in Jesus after witnessing his miracles yet were clearly not saved (John 2:23–24). Here in Acts 8:21 Peter declares: "You have neither part nor lot in this matter," the "matter" being the blessings of the gospel that have come to those in Samaria who believed. "Your heart is not right before God" (v. 21), and "You are in the gall of bitterness and in the bond of iniquity" (v. 23).

There are several other texts that affirm this principle, but I'll only mention two: 1 John 2:19 and Hebrews 3:14.

In 1 John 2:19 John is seeking to expose false teachers in the church who were leading astray the people of God. In verse 19 he indicates that at one time they had been active, vocal participants in the community that professed faith in Christ. They had been immersed in the ministry of the church, were well known among God's people, and until the moment of separation were hardly distinguishable from the rest of Christian society. Here is what John says of them:

> "*They went out from us.*" They went out by either excommunication or voluntary separation (probably the latter); note the sharp distinction between "they" and "us."

> "*but they were not of us.*" In spite of their external membership, they did not share the inner life. "of us" = the spiritual bond of the body of Christ.

> "*for if they had been of us, they would have continued with us.*" If they had in any genuine sense shared the spiritual life of the community of faith, such life would have persevered and produced the fruit of Christlike holiness; again, we see that the test of life and salvation is abiding.

> "*But they went out, that it might become plain that they all are not of us.*" There is a divine purpose in their secession, namely, exposure of those who are mere professors; their departure was their unmasking (cf. 1 Cor. 11:18–19).

John's inescapable point is that continuing or persevering is the sign of the saved, just as apostasy is the evidence of unbelief. Note the emphasis of the phrase "for if they had been of us, *they would have continued with us.*" The presence of genuine faith ("of us") implies (necessitates) perseverance.

The author of Hebrews makes this same point: "For we have come to share in Christ, if indeed we hold our original confidence firm to the end" (Heb. 3:14). He refers to our "original confidence" in Christ, clearly describing the initial act of faith when people claim to have put their trust in Jesus for salvation. If people who profess to have confidence in Christ hold firmly in this faith all the way "to the end" (a likely reference to the end of his life), this proves that they truly "have come to share in Christ."

How can we know whether Charley genuinely shares in Christ, which is to say, is a true child of God? We can know by observing whether he holds that original confidence firm to the end. Notice that the author does not say that if you hold that confidence firm to the end you "will" be one who shares in Christ. He says, rather, that we "have come" [past tense] to share in Christ if we hold our original confidence firm to the end." In other words, it is one's ongoing, future perseverance in faith or their consistent abiding in their confidence in Christ all the way to the end that serves to demonstrate or prove that they genuinely came to share in Christ in the past.

He does not say that if you fail to hold firm your original confidence, it means you once had it but later lost it. Rather, if you fail to hold it, you never had it at all. If Charley does not hold firmly to the end of this "faith" that he claims, it reveals that he never truly shared in Christ in the first place.

Perhaps it will help you see what our author is saying if we state it negatively: "We have *not* come to share in Christ if indeed we do *not* hold our original confidence firm to the end." His point again is that if you are born again and have thus come to share in Christ, you cannot fail to persevere. You will hold your original confidence firm unto the end.

Let's return now to John 15.

We've cited three reasons why this passage does not describe the loss of salvation. We turn now to the fourth by taking note of the phrase "in me" in verse 2. This might refer to genuine salvation, but it is possible that "in me" modifies "bear fruit" rather than "every branch." In other words, instead of rendering the verse "every branch *in me* that does not bear fruit," it could possibly read "every branch not bearing fruit *in me*." The phrase "in me" occurs five additional times in 15:1–7, and in each instance it modifies the verb. Thus it may well be that "in me" emphasizes not the location or place of the branch but the process of fruit bearing.

Fifth, the contrast between verses 2 and 3 supports this view. J. Carl Laney points out that "having just spoken about the removal of fruitless branches, Jesus explained to the disciples that He did not have them in view (v. 3). They were already 'clean' . . . by virtue of their response to Christ's Person and message (cf. 13:10–11). Jesus was giving His disciples instruction that did not represent their own spiritual situation, but had primary application to those to whom they would minister, those who would claim to be Christ's but were not bearing fruit."[4]

Sixth, and finally, let's not forget that Jesus is using an image drawn from horticulture, which requires that we take care not to press the details for more theological information than he intended. Jesus is making the point that *fruitfulness is a necessary and infallible mark of true Christianity.* He uses the picture of a vine to drive home this truth. Where else could a branch be located if not in some way connected with the vine? Jesus could hardly make his point by directing their attention to a bunch of disconnected and isolated branches scattered about on the ground. Jesus is saying that no branch that fails to bear fruit can be thought of as united to him. If you are going to be connected to Jesus, you must bear fruit. Therefore, what else can be done with fruitless branches other than to cut them off and cast them away?

---

[4] J. Carl Laney, "Abiding Is Believing: The Analogy of the Vine in John 15:1–6," *Bibliotheca Sacra* (January–March), 1989: 64.

But we shouldn't press the imagery and draw the theological conclusion that many true Christians fail to bear fruit but are then cut off and suffer eternal condemnation. That is pressing the image beyond what it is intended to teach us.

My conclusion, then, is that this passage does not teach that a born-again Christian can apostatize from the faith and lose his or her salvation. It does teach that it is impossible to bear fruit apart from a life-giving, saving union with Jesus (v. 4) and that it is impossible not to bear fruit when that connection with Jesus truly exists (v. 5). It also teaches that some (many?) who profess to be united to Jesus, who claim to believe him and even "follow" him as so-called disciples, will be revealed by their lack of fruit as spurious and thus subject to eternal judgment.

CONCLUSION

In the controversy over eternal security raised by this passage, it is all too easy to miss what may be the most important thing that Jesus says in it: "Apart from me you can do nothing" (v. 5b).

Some say, "But, Sam, that makes no sense. After all, I do lots of things in life every day without ever thinking of Jesus. So too do all non-Christians. We go to work and put in a solid day at the office. We go to movies and dinner with our spouses and meet in our small groups. What could Jesus possibly mean by saying that apart from him we can do nothing?"

The context tells us precisely what he means. He is talking about bearing fruit. You can bear no meaningful, lasting, eternally significant, life-changing spiritual and moral fruit apart from Jesus. He's talking about authentic transformation in the human heart and meaningful, eternal influence for good in the lives of others. He's talking about those things that truly honor and glorify God and serve to spread his fame throughout the earth.

Jesus is saying that apart from conscious, consistent communion with him, drawing on his presence and power in our lives, we can accomplish nothing of spiritual value. If we want to live in such a way that our lives honor God and help others, we must abide in Christ, which means that we immerse ourselves in his Word. It means we obey his commands. It means we are always prayerful, embedded in Christian community, worshiping Jesus in all of life, and living on mission with him every day.

In the absence of all this, no one can be assured of salvation. As Jesus said, "If you abide in my word, you are truly my disciples" (John 8:31); and, "By this my Father is glorified, that you bear much fruit and so prove to be my disciples" (15:8).

4

THE LOGIC OF LOVE

Love and logic. If you were to ask most people, they'd tell you that one often precludes the other. Logic is all about the mind. Love is all about the heart. Logic is about reason. Love is about relationships. Logic is concerned with principles whereas love is all about passion. Well, in this chapter I'm going to take these two seemingly incompatible items and marry them. What I hope to show is that the security of your salvation in Christ Jesus is grounded in *the logic of love*.

ROMANS 5:6–11

This topic is so practical and helpful to think about because of what it reveals about God. This doctrine is a window into the heart of our heavenly Father. This truth pulls back the curtain on the mystery of God's ways and shines a light into the depths of how he thinks and feels and what his purposes are for you and me. And nowhere is this better seen than in Romans 5:6–11:

> For while we were still weak, at the right time Christ died for the ungodly. For one will scarcely die for a righteous per-son—though perhaps for a good person one would dare even to die—but God shows his love for us in that while we were still sinners, Christ died for us. Since, therefore, we have now been justified by his blood, much more shall we be saved by

him from the wrath of God. For if while we were enemies we were reconciled to God by the death of his Son, much more, now that we are reconciled, shall we be saved by his life. More than that, we also rejoice in God through our Lord Jesus Christ, through whom we have now received reconciliation.

The point of the apostle here is that our hope is as secure as God's love is sincere. We are secure in our salvation as long as God loves us. But what if God should stop loving us? What if something should happen to diminish his passion for his people? Paul's purpose in verses 6–11 is to prove that such will never happen.

The first thing Paul does is answer the question, "For what kind of people did Christ die?" Was it only registered Republicans? Only God-fearing monotheists? Only those whose skin color is identical with ours? Only the wealthy? Only the poor?

Christ did not die for people of a particular political persuasion or socioeconomic-educational status or for those naturally inclined toward God or who express a desire to cease from their enmity against him. In particular, he died for men and women of all races of all levels of social status who together are all weak, ungodly, sinful enemies.

Jesus died for spiritually impotent people (Rom. 3:10–12). He died for people who were helpless to prepare themselves, helpless to prove themselves worthy, helpless to do or think or say anything that might attract God's love. Contrary to the aphorism "God helps those who help themselves," God helps those who are utterly and absolutely helpless.

Jesus died for ungodly people, that is, people who are both unlike God and opposed to God. Jesus died for sinful people. He didn't die for a single righteous person. Jesus died for his enemies. Jesus didn't die for a single friend. He died for rebellious, insolent, haughty, arrogant, self-righteous, repulsive, disobedient, at-war-with-God people.

The kind of people for whom Jesus died is illustrated in verses 7–8. The "righteous" person is the just man, the man governed by duty, the man who meets his obligations, the lawful man who evokes your respect but not necessarily your affection. Paul says that although you might admire such a man and perhaps even provide him a measure of assistance, it is unlikely that you would *die* for him.

The "good" man is the righteous one who is also kind, gentle, and loving, the man who evokes your admiration and affection. For such a man you might be willing to die. Odds are a little more in his favor that someone would step forward to make the ultimate sacrifice on his behalf.

But God demonstrates the depth and quality of his love by sending his Son to die—not for righteous or good men but for weak, ungodly, sinful men who hate him.

What you and I would only reluctantly do for a good man God joyfully and spontaneously did for evil men. Mothers and fathers would gladly die for the sake of their child, but would they die for a person who kidnapped and killed him?

But that is what God did. He didn't send his Son to die for those who loved him or sought him or helped him or served him. He sent his Son to die for his murderers, for those who spit in his face and despised him. So what was it about us that so attracted God that he sent his Son to die? Was it our pleas for help? Our good intentions? A spark of divinity? Our potential? It was nothing.

We must also remember that the cross is the demonstration of God's love for us, not the provocation of it. Christ's love did not procure or obtain the love of God. It was a manifestation of that love. Jesus doesn't stand before the Father pleading, "Oh, Father, I died for them; therefore love them." Rather he declares, "You love them, Father, and that is why I died for them."

My understanding is that God loved us in spite of our unloveliness, not because of our loveliness. Nothing in us stirred God's heart to send his Son. He sent his Son solely because of his character as a loving God. When God contemplated the objects of his redemptive love, he saw only sin, rebellion, enmity, and resistance. The love of God in Christ is magnified in that while we were still sinners, Christ died for us. God saw us as weak and ungodly people, not as treasures. The only thing we stirred in God's heart was wrath. The only thing we incline God to do is judge us eternally. God gave his Son in love solely because of his great and unfathomable determination to love those who were the moral antithesis of himself and the enemies of everything he regards as holy, true, and right.

I've often heard people emphasize our value as treasures and pearls in God's sight, as if that is what moved his heart to send Jesus to die for us. But if that is the case, what becomes of grace? The cross is an expression of grace because those for whom Christ died merited only wrath and hell. If those for whom he died were contemplated as treasures whom God valued, do we not diminish the nature of grace? Do we not, to that degree, merit his atoning sacrifice? If God saw something in us that stirred him to send Jesus for us, the gift of his Son ceases to be grace and becomes a matter of debt.

I've often heard this: "We say to Jesus, 'Who were we that led you to do this for us?' Jesus then says to us, 'You were a treasure hidden to yourself but seen by me.'" But my understanding is that when we ask, "Who were we that led you to do this for us?" the only answer is: "You were hell-deserving rebels who had no claim on anything in me other than to be the recipients of eternal wrath. I did this for you not because you were a treasure or because of anything in you; indeed it was in spite of what was in you. I did this for you solely because of what was in me, namely, sovereign and free and gracious love for those who deserve only to be hated."

Certainly I agree that God saved us in Christ in order that he might make treasures of us, but not because we already were treasures. I fear that some might still think that the reason why God chose to love us in Christ was our loveliness, our value as treasures.

If that were the case, we could no longer speak of the cross as an act of grace.

It was grace, because the cause for it is found wholly in God's good pleasure and decision to shed his love on people whose only distinguishing feature was the fact that they deserved his wrath. When people think about why God smiled on them in the cross of Christ, they should say, "It certainly wasn't because of anything in me. In fact, I should have brought only a frown of judgment to his face. That he should have smiled in redemptive love is traceable only to his sovereign and gracious good pleasure. Thanks be to God that he has chosen to make a treasure out of a moral dung heap."

A Word of Clarification

When I presented these truths in a sermon one day, a few objected to my language. They thought I was saying that human beings lack value in the sight of God, or perhaps, even worse, that humans are in some sense *worthless*. I assured them that this is most certainly not what I intended.

All men and women have value simply by virtue of the fact that they were created in God's image. The image of God in mankind has most assuredly not been altogether erased or destroyed by the fall. That the image of God in man has been severely damaged is recognized by all. Paul even speaks of sanctification as, in one sense, the restoration or renewal of the image of God in us (Col. 3:10; cf. Eph. 4:24). God's handiwork always has value, whether that is the natural creation, angelic beings, or humans. Even Satan has value and worth in the sense that he is a product of God's creative genius. The very fact that we are to care for creation, i.e., the environment, is due to the fact that God made nature and placed us as stewards over it.

However, it is one thing to say that we have value as image bearers; it is altogether another thing to suggest that what moved God to love us and send us his Son to die in our stead was our value. Of course, it was humans, not dogs or carrots or apple trees, for whom

Jesus died. As Hebrews 2 indicates, the Son took upon himself the nature of the children of Abraham, not that of angels or any other order of created being. He did this because it is his desire to commune forever with those in his image. We alone, by virtue of that image, are capable of the sort of self-consciousness, moral responsibility, love, and relational intimacy that are required to enjoy God and thereby glorify him forever. All creation in its own way glorifies God. But humans alone do so by enjoying, delighting in, and finding their ultimate satisfaction in who God is, which is what he created us for. That is why we were the focus of his redemptive work through Jesus rather than rocks or clouds or stars.

However, what stirred the heart of God to send his Son was the free and sovereign choice of love. I don't believe God said, "Well [or perhaps even, "Wow"], these fallen humans are of such worth that I now feel love for them and, based on this worth, I will send Jesus to die for them and redeem them." As I read Scripture, I think God would instead have said, "Well, these fallen humans deserve only my wrath and eternal damnation. They have squandered all that I gave them. They are helpless to do anything that might merit my favor. They are ungodly in the sense that they are both morally unlike me and relationally against me. They are sinful in thought, word, and deed. They are my enemies. But I am determined to glorify myself through them. Therefore, in spite of the fact that they don't deserve anything other than hell, in spite of the fact that if I were to immediately consign every one of them to eternal condemnation and be perfectly just and righteous in doing so, I am going to love them. I am going to choose to have compassion on them. I am going to take these immoral wretches and make them treasures and trophies of my grace." That is, in my opinion, what Scripture says to us, particularly in Romans 5:6–11.

Another part of my sermon that day addressed why our redemption required the sacrifice of the precious and costly blood of Jesus. I believe it is because of the immeasurable heights and holy demands of God's character as just and righteous. The value of God's holiness could be satisfied with nothing less than the life, death, and resurrection of his sinless Son. No other sacrifice would suffice, not because those redeemed are so valuable that an immeasurably high price was required, but because their sin was so evil, and the one against whom they sinned was so gloriously good, that only the blood of Jesus could make amends and fully satisfy the justice of such a God.

Simply put, the great and immeasurably costly price of Christ's blood was required not because of the value of those offending but because of the value of the one offended. Again, this doesn't mean the "offending" don't have any value. But their value is not the reason why so precious a price was required to save them. My point is that nothing in us merited the love that God demonstrated in sending his Son to die for us. I don't see how one can read Romans 5:6–11 and draw any other conclusion. And I believe we can happily affirm this truth without diminishing our value as image bearers or denying the glorious truth that humans are the handiwork of God's marvelous and incalculable creative design.

And Now, the Logic of Love

Now we come to the glorious logic of love. Paul concludes from verses 9–11 that if it is certain that we have been justified by faith in Christ, it is much more certain that we will be delivered from God's wrath in the future.

But on what basis does Paul make this assertion? The technical name for this sort of logical argument is *a fortiori*, i.e., reasoning from the greater to the lesser. If the greater task was God's sending his Son to die for us while we were his enemies, how much easier for him to save us and live for us now that we are his friends? If God loved us as much as he did while we were helpless, sinful, and ungodly, how much more shall he love us now that we are justified, righteous in Christ, adopted as children, and reconciled to his heart?

If ever there were a time for God not to love you, to forsake and abandon you, it would have been while you were unreconciled and at enmity with him. But now you are no longer an alien but a member of God's household, no longer unreconciled but a child, no longer at enmity but in love with the Lord of your life. It is logically and theologically impossible that God should love you less now that you are his child than he loved you when you were his enemy.

When you find yourself depressed and fearful that God has abandoned you, take yourself in hand and shout aloud to your soul: Much more! Much more! Much more! Awaken passion, joy, and peace in your soul with the logic of God's love.

Paul is clear, and we need to hear him: the wrath of God is coming (v. 9). He is referring here to that great day of final judgment. Who or what will rescue us from this coming wrath? The answer is clear from everything Paul has said in these verses: only the love of God can rescue us from the wrath of God. And we know with unshakable assurance that we will never taste the wrath of God because of the logic of love. So let me say it again: if God did the immeasurably greater thing in giving us his Son when we were his bitter and ungodly enemies, *how much more* shall he sustain us in and through his Son now that we have been reconciled to him as friends and children.

Romans 8:31–32

Evidently the apostle Paul thought this theological principle was worth stating yet again, so he returns to it in Romans 8:31–32. "He who did not spare his own Son but gave him up for us all, how will he not also with him graciously give us all things?" (v. 32).[1]

If Paul had merely asked, "*Will* God give us all things?" we might have wondered. We might have said in response: "Well, you know, I need so many things, big things, important things; how can I be

---

[1] I especially recommend the treatment of this passage, extending through the end of Romans 8, in J. I. Packer, *Knowing God* (Downers Grove, IL: InterVarsity, 1993), 258–79.

certain God will provide them? I'm not saying he lacks the power to do so, but what if he lacks the will?"

But look at how Paul phrased the question. The God who Paul says will graciously give us all things is the God who "did not spare his own Son but gave him up for us all." In other words, the God about whom we ask if he will give us all things is the very God, the only God, who has already given us his very own beloved Son, Jesus Christ.

Again we see that since God has done the indescribably great and costly thing—sacrificing his only begotten Son—we may be fully confident that he will do what is by comparison infinitely less.

Why was God's gift of Jesus Christ the greatest thing imaginable? It was the greatest gift primarily because he loves his Son infinitely, his own dear Son. There isn't anything I wouldn't do for my children. I'm often frightened by the depth and intensity of my love for them. It scares me because of the lengths to which I would go to ensure their spiritual, physical, and emotional welfare. Yet my love and affection for them pales in comparison to the passion that God the Father has for God the Son. We're talking about the love that exists between the first and second persons of the divine Trinity. We're talking about infinite love, omnipotent love, eternal love.

He didn't send an angel into this world clothed in flesh to suffer at the hands of evil men and be nailed to a cross. God didn't send the archangel Michael or Gabriel. It wasn't one of the four living creatures from the book of Revelation. It was his precious, only-begotten, eternal Son.

The second reason why this was such an unimaginable expression of love and sacrifice is that his Son did not deserve to die. His Son deserved worship and honor and praise, not spitting and beating and scorn and, worst of all, the wrath of God himself.

The point is this: if God would do the greatest thing for you, he will certainly do all lesser things. You live in fear that God won't do all lesser things and provide all you need to stay faithful to him, but in comparison with giving Christ Jesus, it's a breeze. Giving you all things is easy. This is the unbreakable, unshakeable logic of heaven.

Do you remember pay phones, those telephone booths (like those into which Clark Kent went to change into Superman)? Think of those days. Now imagine if Bill Gates were to give you a $5 billion cashier's check, arranged that you wouldn't have to pay one penny of tax, and drafted a legally binding document that guarantees you can do with this money anything you please. Are you getting the picture? Now, suppose you wanted to call your spouse to tell her the good news and asked, "Mr. Gates, may I borrow a dime to make a phone call?" Would it make any sense if he were to say no? If Mr. Gates was joyfully generous in giving you $5 billion, how much more would he be willing to throw in a dime that you might share this great news with your spouse? Such is the reasoning or logic of Paul in Romans 5 and 8.

Let's stay with verse 32 and Paul's argument a bit longer. Negatively, God did not spare his own Son. Parents, we spare our children when we refrain from inflicting on them all the discipline that their disobedience calls for. Judges spare criminals when they reduce or suspend a sentence. But this is precisely what God did not do with Jesus. He did not withhold one stroke of his holy wrath in punishing Jesus for what we have done. No mitigation of the judgment, no lessening of the penalty, no suspension of the sentence, no leniency at all.

Positively, he "gave him up" for us all, or better still, he "delivered" him up. Who delivered up Jesus, and why? Was it Judas Iscariot, and did he do it for thirty pieces of silver? No. Perhaps the ultimate culprit was Herod, motivated by a perceived but mistaken fear that Jesus was a political threat to his power. No. Was it the Jewish religious leaders who did it out of jealousy? No. Was it Pontius Pilate, who did it from fear of the crowds? No. It was God the Father, and he did it because of love for you and me.

Therefore—pause and saturate your soul with the glorious logic of love—*therefore* God will do what is by comparison infinitely easier. He will give us all things we need for spiritual success. Whatever is necessary for you to make it to the end of life still faithful and trusting Christ, God will give you. Whatever is necessary for you to be conformed to the image of his Son and to resist temptation, he will give you.

What exactly does Paul mean by "all things" in verse 32? There are things we may not receive that we mistakenly think God ought to give us such as better health, better job, better husband, better wife, longer life, more respect from peers, or more fame. By "all things," Paul means everything essential to knowing, loving, and enjoying God more. Everything you need to find complete satisfaction for your soul in God, and joy for your heart in God, he will most assuredly supply. He has in mind everything you need to retain your faith and trust in him, everything that is required so you won't apostatize from the faith.

God will not withhold anything essential for your eternal enjoyment of him.

Think about what kind of person you would be and the kind of life you would live if you really believed verse 32. You know that Jesus calls on us to deny ourselves, take up our cross, and follow him daily. You know that he calls on us to lay up treasure in heaven and not upon earth. You know that he warns us that if we follow him, we will suffer persecution, whether slander or gossip or injustice or mockery or imprisonment or death. You know that we are called by our Lord to embrace humility, meekness, and gentleness and to pursue purity of life.

So why don't we do it? The biggest reason is fear. We are afraid of being stranded, left to ourselves, trampled upon, exploited,and left with nothing. The bottom line is that we are not persuaded that God really will provide us with all we need to live the life he's called us to live. Our fear is fueled by unbelief.

And if all that weren't enough, don't overlook the word "graciously" in verse 32. Let me tell you why this is so important. People think, *Yes, he'll give me what I need so long as I work for it, so long as I pay him for it, so long as I promise him I'll never screw up again, so long as I live a perfect life, and so long as I never doubt him or deny him.*

If that were the case, then whatever God gives you in return for what you've given him would be the payment of a debt, not a gift of grace. When he says that God "graciously" or "freely" gives us all we need to stay secure and safe and joyful and peaceful in our salvation, he means that it has nothing to do with what we do or give or say. This "giving" of "all things" is not God's reimbursing you. It is not God's fulfilling an obligation. It is God in sovereign freedom freely and graciously, with no strings attached, giving you and me what we don't deserve.

That doesn't mean that upon receiving "all things" we shouldn't live good and godly lives or that we shouldn't be thankful and that we shouldn't seek to honor him in all we do. Of course we should. But again these are the fruit of his graciously giving us all things, not the condition on which it is given.

CONCLUSION

Do logic and love conflict? Must we choose between one or the other? No. This is a truth that virtually pulsates with passion. This is unbreakable, unshakable, irrefutable logic that ought to send spiritual and emotional and even physical shock waves through every fiber and cell of your being.

If you can hear Paul say this, and it doesn't rattle your bones with a spine-tingling, joy-filled, heartfelt assurance of your salvation now and forever in eternity, I don't know what else I can say to you. I don't know what else Paul can say to you.

5

INSEPARABLE:
NOW AND FOREVER

Doubt or uncertainty isn't always bad.[1] It can be productive when it drives us into deeper prayer and study and investigation. If we are absolutely convinced about everything, beyond the shadow of a doubt, we face the even bigger problem of arrogance and pride. Doubt humbles. It reminds us that we are finite and that our knowledge is always subject to improvement and increase.

But doubt can also be crippling in a way that undermines our relationship with God. If we are constantly doubting his Word or wondering if he will fulfill his promises or are cynical of his stated intentions, it's hard to grow spiritually.

I've known many who are tormented by fears that God can't be as good as he portrays himself in Scripture. Some experience a gnawing anxiety about whether Jesus was really God and whether he can be trusted with their lives. But the worst and most crippling kind of doubt is when children of God live in fear and anxiety over the forgiveness of their sins and the security and safety of their soul in Christ.

In Colossians 2:2 Paul prayed for the Christians in that city that they might "reach all the riches of full assurance of understanding."

---

[1] Some of what follows has been adapted from my book *The Hope of Glory: 100 Daily Meditations on Colossians* (Wheaton, IL: Crossway, 2008). Used by permission of Crossway.

Let me say a few things about this statement. First, full assurance is a very real possibility for us. That doesn't mean we will never again scratch our heads in bewilderment or wonder if a biblical statement can really mean what it seems to mean. But it does mean there is a degree of certainty concerning the most basic and foundational truths in Scripture that is attainable in this life, most important of which is the assurance that we are truly the children of God and that nothing can separate us from his love.

I don't think it's possible for us, at least not this side of heaven, to banish every wayward thought that runs counter to what God says in his Word. But that doesn't mean we can't experience what Paul refers to as "full assurance."

Second, this assurance or conviction concerning the truth of the gospel is characterized by "riches" or "wealth" (Col. 2:2). There is great treasure in knowing that the gospel of Christ is true and that we are truly and forever saved and reconciled to God, which is Paul's way of saying that indescribable blessing and unfathomable joy and ineffable peace fill the human heart when it attains full assurance of all that God has made known of himself.

Third, and perhaps most important, look closely again at Paul's words: "full assurance of understanding." We could as easily render this, "full assurance that comes from understanding" or "unshakeable confidence that is produced by knowledge."

The point is that assurance is a function of knowledge. Our confidence in God's promises is subject to varying degrees depending on the depth of understanding we have attained in the things of God. Not everyone is equally confident about what God has revealed to us in Christ, because not everyone is equally informed.

When knowledge is made an end in itself, prized for its own sake, it breeds arrogance and pride, and it "puffs up" (1 Cor. 8:1). But when a person humbly applies himself to the pursuit of knowledge and looks to the power of the Spirit to bring illumination and insight, the wealth of his assurance increases and the riches of confident hope expand.

Although we can have full assurance of eternal life the moment we trust in Christ (John 3:16), our confidence grows and intensifies in direct proportion to our cognitive grasp of the broad expanse of what God has revealed. Knowledge is the soil in which the seeds of peace and certainty germinate.

As our understanding deepens, so too do the peace and tranquility of "knowing that we know" that God is true and will do what he has said he will do.

One of my goals is to enable you to *defeat doubt* by immersing your mind in the Word of God. This is the ordained means by which the Spirit indelibly imprints on your heart the joyful and undeniable assurance that what God has said, God will do. That is why we are spending so much time digging so deeply into these passages that describe the love and grace of Christ and the unshakable security we have in him.

ROMANS 8:1[2]

"There is therefore now no condemnation for those who are in Christ Jesus" (Rom. 8:1).

There is a poetic beauty in the way Romans 8 both begins and ends. It begins with *no condemnation in Christ* (v. 1) and ends with *no separation from Christ* (v. 39). I want you to see three things Paul says about our eternal life and the forgiveness of sins.

First, note what Paul says about the nature of the gift: "no condemnation." The word *condemnation* is ominous. We hear it used in a courtroom, for example, where the accused has come under sentence of *condemnation* for some heinous crime, or when the president *condemns* the terrorist attack on our embassy in Libya, or

---

[2] As we approach this passage, the best advice I can give you is to stop reading this book and examine two sermons by John Piper: "No Condemnation in Christ Jesus, Part 1," September 9, 2001; and "No Condemnation in Christ Jesus, Part 2," September 30, 2001, http://www.desiringgod.org.

when survivors of the Russian Gulag *condemn* many in the West for apparently not speaking out against Stalin's agenda, or even when a dilapidated building is *condemned* by the city and consigned to ultimate destruction.

No less forceful is the use of the word in Scripture where it refers to the liability or exposure of sinners to the penal sanctions of divine law or their vulnerability to divine wrath. Such condemnation is the antithesis of justification. If to be justified is to stand boldly before God because we are declared righteous in his sight through faith alone, to be condemned is to cower with fear because we are unrighteous and worthy of death.

When we think of that word and all it entails: the loss of hope, fear of the future, shattered dreams, painful separation, and so on, Paul's declaration suddenly begins to reverberate in our hearts with a power and force that make it feel as if we are going to explode with joy, exuberance, and gratitude.

This is the sort of good news that takes your breath away, to think that those in Christ Jesus have no valid reason to ever again experience fear or apprehension about their relationship with God or their eternal destiny. That doesn't mean they *won't* experience such fear. It does mean there is no valid reason why they *should*. Martyn Lloyd-Jones explains:

> There are many who misunderstand this. They seem to think of the Christian as a man who, if he confesses his sin and asks for forgiveness, is forgiven. At that moment he is not under condemnation. But then if he should sin again he is back once more under condemnation. Then he repents and confesses his sin again, and asks for pardon, and he is cleansed once more. So to them the Christian is a man who is constantly passing from one state to the other; back and forth; condemned, not condemned. Now that, according to the Apostle, is a wholly mistaken notion, and a complete failure to understand the position. The Christian is a man who can never be condemned;

he can never come into a state of condemnation again. "No condemnation!" The Apostle is not talking about his experience, but about his position, his standing, his status; he is in a position in which, being justified, he can never again come under condemnation. That is the meaning of this word "no." It means "Never."[3]

Why is this declaration by Paul so important? First, nothing paralyzes as powerfully as guilt and shame. Financial worries, family struggles, and physical pain are hindrances and create pressure in life. But nothing makes life feel as if it's not worth getting up for quite like guilt, shame, and condemnation. It's also important because, as has often been said, the only sin we can defeat is a sin that has been forgiven. There are natural ways and homemade remedies for overcoming bad habits: therapy, self-help formulas, willpower, twelve-step programs, and the like. But they often produce self-righteousness, not God's righteousness.

Forgiveness of sin, the removal of guilt, and the consequent declaration "No condemnation" must precede our battle against sin if it is to empower our battle against sin. God's declaration of "No condemnation" must come first and thus enable and energize our transformation into righteousness-loving, Christ-exalting people. The divine declaration must come before the human transformation. Being right with God must precede doing right for God.

Second, don't overlook what Paul says about who enjoys this blessing. Paul does not say Christians are free from condemnation because they are sinless; it is because they are in Christ. "No condemnation" is not a universal blessing. It is reserved for those who have been united spiritually with Christ through faith. We must be careful to resist the false sentimentality that beckons us to give false assurance to non-Christians simply because they are sincere, nice, religious, or believe in God.

---

[3] D. M. Lloyd-Jones, *Romans: An Exposition of Chapters 7.1–8.4, The Law: Its Functions and Limits* (Grand Rapids, MI: Zondervan, 1975), 271.

To be "in Christ" by faith alone means, among other things, that his righteousness has been reckoned or imputed to you. It means you are united with him in a spiritual covenant. It means there is an almost indefinable mystical oneness or spiritual fellowship with the Lord that you share every moment of life. To put it as simply as possible, to be "in Christ" means you are saved by him and are in vibrant spiritual union with him.

You may find it mildly amusing that some Greek manuscripts add a qualifying phrase to verse 1: ". . . who walk not after the flesh but after the Spirit" (see KJV). Most likely this was due to some early scribe who couldn't bring himself to let verse 1 stand alone, perhaps fearing that to do so would encourage people to exploit God's grace to justify their sin. So he took the last phrase of verse 4 and appended it to verse 1 to soften the force of Paul's statement, as if to say: "Oh, sure, there's no condemnation so long as you're walking in the Spirit and not after the flesh." But when are we ever walking sufficiently and consistently in the Spirit so as to escape condemnation? If our freedom from condemnation is suspended on or conditioned by or only as good as our success in not indulging the flesh, we are hopeless. It will never happen this side of heaven.

Third, and finally, when is it true? It is true now. Not when we get older. Not when we get more mature. Not when we overcome all sinful habits. Not when we get past being hurt by others. Not when all our bills are paid. Not when we get a new job. Not when we've lost that extra thirty pounds that threaten our health. Not when we learn more of the Bible. Not when people start treating us nicely and with respect. Not when we get the praise and public adulation we think we deserve. Not when our enemies stop persecuting us. Not when the wrongs against us have been put right. Not when we've been vindicated. Not when we stop making fools of ourselves in public. Not when we stop failing God. Not when we break free of all addictions. Not when we've stopped doubting God. It is now!

ROMANS 8:28–30

> We know that for those who love God all things work together
> for good, for those who are called according to his purpose. For
> those whom he foreknew he also predestined to be conformed
> to the image of his Son, in order that he might be the firstborn
> among many brothers. And those whom he predestined he
> also called, and those whom he called he also justified, and
> those whom he justified he also glorified.

It is important to remember that everyone who believes in the Bible
believes in predestination and election. The issue isn't whether you
have a doctrine of election but what kind of doctrine you have. The
verb "to choose" or "to elect" is used twenty-two times in the New
Testament, seven of which refer to election, salvation, or eternal life.
The noun "elect" also occurs twenty-two times, seventeen of which
refer to men and women chosen or elected to eternal life. The noun
"election" occurs seven times, all with reference to salvation. The
verb "to predestine" occurs six times, four of which refer to men
being predestined to salvation (see Eph. 1:5, 11).

It's not my goal in this chapter to address the nature of election
but rather to observe the unbreakable and eternal chain of God's
saving purpose for us in Christ. I say it is "eternal" because it spans
eternity past into eternity future. It starts with divine foreknowledge before the foundation of the world and consummates in glorification in the age to come.

The first link in this eternal chain of salvation is *foreknowledge*.
I'm not going to address all the many theories of what this means.
Based on the use of this language in both Old and New Testaments,
my understanding is that the verb "to know" refers to something
far more than intellectual understanding. It is used as a virtual syn-
onym for love. It means to set one's affection upon or to highly regard or delight in someone with peculiar interest (see Gen. 18:19; Ex.

2:25; Pss. 1:6; 144:3; Jer. 1:5; Amos 3:2; Hos. 13:5; Matt. 7:23; 1 Cor. 8:3; Gal. 4:9; 2 Tim. 2:19; 1 John 3:1).

In an earlier chapter we looked at Matthew 7:23, where Jesus reveals his future response to false disciples at the last judgment: "I never knew you; depart from me." As Baugh has pointed out, "Clearly, mere intellectual cognition is ruled out as the meaning of 'know' here, since it is precisely Jesus' knowledge of their real motives and covenantal status and commitments that leads to their condemnation. Rather, he says that these people never had covenantal relations with him; the Good Shepherd did not know them as his sheep, and they did not know him (John 10:14)."[4]

Thus, to foreknow is to forelove. Paul isn't merely saying that God thought about you in eternity past, but that he loved you before the worlds were formed. That God foreknew us is but another way of saying that he set his gracious and merciful regard upon us, that he knew us from eternity past with a sovereign and distinguishing delight. God's foreknowledge is an active, creative work of divine love. It is not bare prevision that merely recognizes a difference between men who believe and men who do not. God's foreknowledge creates that difference.

The second link in this eternal chain of salvation is *predestination*. Predestination and foreknowledge are not synonymous. Foreknowledge focuses attention on the distinguishing love of God whereby people are elected. Predestination points to the decision God made of what he intended to do with those whom he foreknew (see Acts 4:28; Eph. 1:5, 11). Predestination is that act in eternity past in which God decreed that those on whom he had set his saving love would inherit eternal life.

The third link in the eternal chain of salvation is *calling*. This is not merely an invitation to come to Christ. This calling is the power-

---

[4] S. M. Baugh, "The Meaning of Foreknowledge," in *Still Sovereign: Contemporary Perspectives on Election, Foreknowledge, and Grace*, ed. Thomas R. Schreiner and Bruce A. Ware (Grand Rapids, MI: Baker, 2000), 194.

ful work of the Holy Spirit by which he effectively secures a response in the sinner's heart. We know that, because all who are called are also justified. Paul doesn't say that only some of those called are justified. Paul "fuses the called and justified together so that those who have experienced calling have also inevitably received the blessing of justification."[5]

The fourth link in the eternal chain of salvation is *justification*. Justification is God's legal declaration that the righteousness of his Son, Jesus Christ, has been imputed or reckoned to us so that we stand in his presence fully accepted and forgiven by faith alone.

The fifth and final link in the eternal chain of salvation is *glorification*. Note the use of the past tense in describing glorification (see v. 30). This may seem strange insofar as we are told in Romans 8:18–25 that glorification is still future. Paul clearly wants to emphasize the fact that our glorification is so sure, so securely set and sealed in the mind and purpose and predestined plan of God that it may be spoken of as having already occurred.

Now, here is what I especially want you to see: each link in this eternal chain of salvation is coextensive with every other link. Paul makes clear that the objects of God's saving activity are the same from start to finish. *Those whom* he foreknew, not one more or one less, *these* also he predestined. And *those whom* he predestined, not one more or one less, *these* also he called. And *those whom* he called, not one more or one less, *these* also he justified. And *those whom* he justified, not one more or one less, *these* also he glorified. There is a continuity in the recipients of salvation from divine foreknowledge in eternity past all the way through glorification in eternity future.

The same point can be made with even greater clarity by asking of Paul a series of questions that starts with the end and works back to the beginning:

---

[5] Thomas R. Schreiner, *Romans*, Baker Exegetical Commentary on the New Testament (Grand Rapids, MI: Baker, 1998), 451.

Q: "Paul, who is finally and fully glorified? Who will stand be-
    fore God fully transformed and forever made like Jesus?"
A: "All those who were justified."
Q: "But who are the justified?"
A: "All those who were called."
Q: "Okay, then, who are the called?"
A: "All those whom God predestined."
Q: "One more question, Paul: Who has been predestined?"
A: "All those whom he foreknew."

So, how many did God lose in the process? Not one. All whom
he foreknew in eternity past will ultimately be glorified in eternity
future. Not one is lost. Not one. No one who is foreknown fails to be
predestined. And no one who is predestined fails to be called. And
no one who is called fails to be justified. And no one who is justified
fails to be glorified.

Romans 8:31–39

Following the great chain of salvation that spans the ages and secures the eternal destiny of all whom God, from the beginning, foreknew, Paul closes his argument with this glorious declaration:

> What then shall we say to these things? If God is for us, who
> can be against us? He who did not spare his own Son but gave
> him up for us all, how will he not also with him graciously give
> us all things? Who shall bring any charge against God's elect?
> It is God who justifies. Who is to condemn? Christ Jesus is the
> one who died—more than that, who was raised—who is at the
> right hand of God, who indeed is interceding for us. Who shall
> separate us from the love of Christ? Shall tribulation, or dis-
> tress, or persecution, or famine, or nakedness, or danger, or
> sword? As it is written,

> "For your sake we are being killed all the day long;
> we are regarded as sheep to be slaughtered."

No, in all these things we are more than conquerors through him who loved us. For I am sure that neither death nor life, nor angels nor rulers, nor things present nor things to come, nor powers, nor height nor depth, nor anything else in all creation, will be able to separate us from the love of God in Christ Jesus our Lord. (Rom. 8:31–39)

If there is an overriding, all-consuming fear people have when it comes to the security of their salvation, it's sin. How many times have you heard, as I have, "But my sins are simply too numerous. I keep doing the same stupid, selfish things over and over and over again. When I think of how ungrateful I am, how prone I am to repeat past failures, how prideful and lustful and weak and addicted I am, I find it almost impossible to believe that a God worth his salt would bother to put up with me any longer and continue to invest his energy in my life."

In response, Paul doesn't say that people won't charge us with wrongdoing. They do it all the time! He's not suggesting that Satan won't make every effort to condemn us by bringing before God and our consciences the many ways we fall short. But it is the charges that fall short. All such accusations are to no avail, but not because we are innocent of what they accuse us of. In fact, we are probably guilty of a lot more than what they can think of or find time to mention. They are to no avail because "Christ Jesus is the one who died" for us (v. 34a).

The penalty that those sins call for, whether they be past, present, or future, has already been paid in full. How can anyone condemn you when Christ has already been condemned in your place? What is left for you to suffer? What guilt or penalty remains that might damage your relationship with God?

And it doesn't stop there. Jesus not only died but was raised from the dead to testify to the sufficiency and perfection of what he accomplished for you on the cross. And he not only was raised from the dead but was exalted to the right hand of God the Father, the place of supremacy and authority and honor and power.

But he was exalted not only to demonstrate his power and authority but also so that he might intercede on your behalf (v. 34b). Each time an accusation is brought against you, Jesus turns to the Father and says: "I was reckoned guilty for that sin. I died for it. Your justice has been satisfied." Over and over and over and over again.

This is the basis on which Paul declares in verse 33b, "It is God who justifies." God declares that you are righteous in his sight, no matter how loudly your enemies say you are guilty, no matter how viciously Satan attacks you, no matter how painfully your conscience screams in protest. It is God who justifies you. Who, then, can possibly bring a charge against you that might stick?

And in what condition were you when God did this? According to Romans 4:5, God justifies the "ungodly." God passed a favorable sentence on your behalf in full view of your moral failures and shortcomings. God justified you with his eyes wide open. He knew the very worst about you at the time he accepted you for Jesus's sake. God didn't wait until you were godly and then justify you on the basis of what you've achieved. He looked at you in full and exhaustive awareness of every sin you would ever commit, and because of what Jesus achieved, he declared you righteous in his sight.

For some of you, I suspect that may still not be enough. You still live in fear that God's love won't last. You are still terrified that something somewhere at some time will wrench you from God's loving embrace. That's why Paul writes what he does in 8:35–39, when he addresses that gnawing fear in your soul that on some day, in some way, Jesus will stop loving you and say, "I'm fed up. I've given you every opportunity, every benefit of the doubt. It's over. Get out of my sight!"

Perhaps you think this way because others said they would never cease loving you but finally did. Why should God be any different from them? So here Paul goes to great lengths to drive home the point. Look carefully down this list.

Tribulation awaits. *Perhaps one day when I'm suffering some trial or persecution I won't respond the way I should. I'll get angry at God or bitter or curse his name. Maybe tribulation will separate me from the love of God in Christ.* No!

What about distress? Might the inner turmoil, the emotional anxiety, the doubts and fears and despair I so often feel lead to God's abandonment of me? No!

But I'm afraid of persecution and how I might buckle under the pressure. Will what others can do to me—their words, rejection, and physical abuse—separate me from the love of God in Christ? No!

There are so many other threats to my well-being: famine, nakedness, danger, and sword. If I should ever go hungry or without clothing or I'm exposed to untold dangers and threats or perhaps even killed, slaughtered as just so many sheep, does that mean God has abandoned me and cut me off from his love in Christ Jesus? No!

Far from it. "In all these things"—all of them, every single one—"we are more than conquerors." It is in them, not by avoiding them or being spared the devastation they bring, but right smack-dab in the middle of them, that we conquer through Christ.

It is "through him who loved us" that the conquering comes. It isn't our courage, our resolve, or our endurance or determination; it's through the presence of Christ at all times and on the basis of what he has accomplished that we conquer. It is not our hold on him but his hold on us that enables us to stand securely through the very worst of times and trials.

As if to hammer the final nail into the coffin of our doubts and fears, Paul lists every conceivable threat to the love of God for us. Neither death nor life can separate you from him. Far from death being able to sever you from his love, it only serves to bring you into his glorious presence. Of course, Paul has in mind not only death itself but also the variety of ways in which it might come upon you. Thus neither cancer nor a car wreck, neither diabetes nor drowning, and no manner of life's end, whether swiftly by martyrdom or slowly in a nursing home, can put an end to the love God has for you in Jesus.

Nothing that life might throw your way can cut you off from his affection. Neither tragedy nor triumph, neither success nor failure—nothing you encounter or experience during your earthly sojourn has the power to undermine God's commitment or overthrow his purpose in bringing you safely into his eternal kingdom.

Neither the holy angels who do God's bidding nor the demonic rulers who oppose his will have the power to threaten your security in Christ. No spiritual power, whether good or evil, can separate you from God's love in Christ.

Neither can things present nor things to come. Nothing now, nothing new, nor anything that may come your way in the future can terminate your relationship with Christ.

No powers. No supernatural force, no miraculous event, nothing—no matter how strong it may seem—can separate you from Christ.

Neither can height nor depth. Nothing above, nothing below, whether from heaven or hell, can disrupt the relationship you have with God.

Nor can anything else in all creation. This final phrase is designed to close down any possible loopholes. No being, no thing, no event, nothing that is or ever will be, not even yourself (after all, you are a created thing) will be able to separate you from the love of Christ.

But what about God himself? He's not created. He's the creator. So maybe he'll separate you from the love of Christ.

The whole point of Paul's argument in Romans 8 is to reassure you that God is on your side and eternally for you. God is for us (not against us), according to Romans 8:31. God will give you everything you need to stay in his love, according to Romans 8:32. And according to Romans 8:33, God will not accuse you; after all, he is the one who justifies you.

CONCLUSION

In 1984 our daughter Melanie was about to turn six, and all she wanted for her birthday was to go with her parents to the Texas State Fair. We were living in Dallas at the time and didn't want to disappoint her. However, the city had been filled with disturbing reports of young children being snatched while playing in their backyards. I can still recall reading in the *Dallas Morning News* a warning to all parents who planned on taking their children to the fair. They were instructed to keep their children close at hand and not let them wander off along the midway. We took it to heart.

The fair was an incredibly entertaining event, especially for a six-year-old girl who wanted to jump on every ride and eat everything she could lay her hands on. As we ventured down the midway, Melanie constantly struggled to break free of my grip on her hand. She was first drawn to the Ferris wheel and then to a game of darts and after that to the bumper cars and then to the booth selling cotton candy. She grew increasingly frustrated by my refusal to let her run free. But I assured her again and again that there wasn't the slightest chance that I would ever let go of her hand, no matter how energetically she pulled to break free or how loudly she complained about being kept by my side. Although she was a precocious child, I don't think she fully grasped my fatherly commitment. She likely interpreted my refusal to let her run wild as the fearful and anxious strategy of an overly protective and controlling parent whose primary aim was to rob her of the joys she otherwise might experience.

After more than two hours of this tug-of-war Melanie showed no signs of giving up. If anything, her stubborn little six-year-old heart had intensified in the determination to have her way along the midway, her daddy's persistent grip notwithstanding. My question for you is this: What would you have thought of me had I said to her, "Fine! I've had enough of your nonsense. If you want to get yourself kidnapped and abused, go ahead. Have at it. I'm done with you. Your refusal to be grateful for my loving protection has worn me down"— spoken in a disillusioned tone as I let go of her hand and watched passively as she wandered into a potentially deadly crowd. I know what you would have thought, as I would have thought of you if it were your child: *What an incredibly unloving and weak-willed father! I can't believe your alleged devotion to your child and your purported concern for her welfare could so easily dissipate under the pressure she imposed on you. What a jerk! If possible, I'd bring charges against you and make sure you suffered the full penal extent of the law.*

I can assure you that no matter how frustrated or exhausted or disappointed I may have grown with her efforts to break free, nothing could have induced me to let go of her hand. And remember that I'm a fallen, selfish, and sinful man. Yet, my depravity notwithstanding, I would never, by no means ever, let go of my child and release her into a potentially dangerous crowd of strangers.

I'm sure you can see where I'm heading with this. If I, being evil, am committed to the ultimate safety and welfare of my child, how much more is your heavenly Father, being good, committed to yours? If I find it inconceivable to even remotely consider the option of abandoning my child, how much less is it a possibility that your heavenly Father would ever dream of abandoning you? If I was willing to do everything imaginable to keep my little girl safe from life-threatening circumstances, including patiently enduring her incessant whining and lack of gratitude for such efforts, how much more will your heavenly Father do whatever is required to keep you safely and savingly embraced in his arms?

It's important to remember one additional difference. As we noted in Romans 8:30–39, God the Father has already done the greatest thing imaginable and made the most costly sacrifice possible to secure our eternal safety. He has crucified his Son in our stead.

He spared him not. He gave him up for us all. Thus when it comes to keeping a tight grip on our souls as we encounter the many threats and attacks and temptations of life, he will not decline to do what is immeasurably less. Of this you can be certain, and in it you may rest assured: your loving and gracious heavenly Father will never let go of your hand; he will never, by no means ever, leave you or forsake you, or ever allow you to leave or forsake him.

6

GOD WILL SUSTAIN YOU TO THE END

As we continue our investigation of what the Bible says about eternal security, we come next to Paul's Corinthian correspondence. It's important to remember that Paul's relationship to the Corinthian church was a rocky one, but not because he lacked love for them or they for him. It was due to the presence in Corinth of an influential group of false apostles and false teachers who promoted themselves by undermining Paul. Sadly, some of the Corinthians had begun to believe their lies. In addition, some of those in Corinth, under the influence of these false teachers, had not fully cut ties with their pagan and idolatrous background. They were attempting to walk with a foot in both worlds—one in the church and the other in the secular, immoral world of ancient Greece.

But one thing is clear in both letters: Paul loved these people with a deep and abiding passion. He had led most of them to the Lord, and he longed for his children in the faith to walk in the joy and peace that comes with faith in Jesus.

1 CORINTHIANS 1:4–9

I give thanks to my God always for you because of the grace of God that was given you in Christ Jesus, that in every way you were enriched in him in all speech and all knowledge—even as

the testimony about Christ was confirmed among you—so that
you are not lacking in any gift, as you wait for the revealing of
our Lord Jesus Christ, who will sustain you to the end, guiltless
in the day of our Lord Jesus Christ. God is faithful, by whom
you were called into the fellowship of his Son, Jesus Christ our
Lord. (1 Cor. 1:4–9)

This is one of the clearest and most striking declarations of God's
commitment to preserve and protect his children all the way
through to the end when Jesus returns. Savor the flavor of so sweet
a promise of God's love for his people, and then swallow it and let it
nourish, enrich, and strengthen your soul.

First, this is unmistakably a promise, not a wish, not a let's-hope-
it-all-turns-out-okay sort of affirmation. Paul says that Jesus Christ
"will" sustain you—not *might* sustain you, not *may* sustain you, not
he'll-give-it-his-best-shot-but-who-knows-if-he-can-pull-it-off sort
of expectation.

Second, the sustaining is something Jesus does. He will "sustain" you. When you feel weak and don't think you can hold on for
another second, when you are convinced that eternal doom awaits
you around the corner, when you fear that God has had it up to his
eyeballs with your failures and faults, recall that Christ promises to
sustain his people.

You should know that the Greek verb translated "sustain"
here in verse 8 is the same verb translated "confirmed" in verse 6.
There Paul declares that "the testimony about Christ was *confirmed*
among" them. That is to say, the gospel was made known, and its
truth was ratified in their presence. Here in verse 8, he uses this verb
to declare that God guarantees that all who embrace that gospel will
stand guiltless before God on the final day. Paul is telling us that our
security in God's love is as solid, sure, and unwavering as the truth
and power of the gospel itself.

Third, this sustaining goes on "to the end" (v. 8). This is clearly a reference to the second coming of Christ at the close of history. In verse 7 he referred to the end as "the revealing of our Lord Jesus Christ," an unmistakable reference to his return, and in verse 8 the "end" is identical with "the day of our Lord Jesus Christ," which all acknowledge is the coming of Christ to consummate his kingdom. The point is that Jesus isn't committed to strengthening and sustaining you only for a short season, only so long as you earn your keep, so to speak. He is committed to keeping and preserving you to the very end.

Fourth, he will sustain us "guiltless," without reproach or moral stain. On the day when Jesus returns, he will present all his people utterly guilt free in the presence of his Father.

He is able to do this but not because you and I live sinless lives between now and then and earn a verdict of innocent. He has imputed his righteousness to us through faith, and in that righteousness we will stand at the final judgment day. Paul is saying here what he said in Romans 8:31–34, that no one can bring a successful accusation against God's people because Christ died and has been raised. That is the basis on which God justifies us. So who is it that condemns? If you trust in Jesus as your treasure, in God's sight, right now, you are guiltless. And you will remain guiltless in his sight right up until, through, and eternally beyond the end because the verdict passed on your behalf will never be overturned. I know that because Paul just said it.

Fifth, and finally, we can be sure of this because "God is faithful" (v. 9). It is the faithfulness of God that guarantees you will be sustained and established guiltless both now and forever. God has made promises to us. He has declared that no one can separate us from the love of Christ. He has made clear that no one can snatch us out of his hand. If God were unworthy of our trust, if he had a record of breaking his promises, we'd have a problem. But listen to Paul: "God is faithful." This God, who called you into fellowship with

Jesus, his Son, is the same God who through Jesus will sustain you to the end.

We are eternally secure in our salvation not because *we* are faithful but because *God* is. He is reliable. He is trustworthy. He is true to himself and will never fail to fulfill what he has promised.

Let's not forget that Paul's original audience here was the Corinthians. That's right—those stumbling, bumbling Christians in Corinth. He makes this unwavering declaration regarding a people whose behavior is anything but blameless and guiltless. Notwithstanding their struggles and setbacks and sins, notwithstanding the often severe rebukes that Paul points in their direction, he reassures them that God will sustain them all the way to the end so that they will stand guiltless in his presence on the day Jesus returns.

1 CORINTHIANS 11:27–32

> Whoever, therefore, eats the bread or drinks the cup of the Lord in an unworthy manner will be guilty concerning the body and blood of the Lord. Let a person examine himself, then, and so eat of the bread and drink of the cup. For anyone who eats and drinks without discerning the body eats and drinks judgment on himself. That is why many of you are weak and ill, and some have died. But if we judged ourselves truly, we would not be judged. But when we are judged by the Lord, we are disciplined so that we may not be condemned along with the world. (1 Cor. 11:27–32)

If we are going to fully grasp how this passage applies to our security in Christ, we must understand the context in which it was written. The problem Paul is addressing here was provoked by the fact that some in Corinth were partaking of the Lord's Table in "an unworthy manner." Let's begin by noting what that does not mean. Ernest Kevan is helpful in this regard:

So many true-hearted believers have been disturbed by a mis-understanding of this. It is said that if you feel ashamed and crestfallen and depressed because of your failure and sin that therefore you must not come [to the Lord's Table]. Oh no! That is the right way to come. To take the Lord's Supper unworthily is to take it without regard to its true worth [not yours]. To do it unworthily is to come complacently, to come light-heartedly, to come without a care about your own sin and your shame. But to be burdened with your sin, even to be weighed down with a sense of your guilt and utter unworthiness—that is to take the Lord's Supper worthily. Only in this spirit do you truly reckon it at its worth.[1]

We also need to keep in mind that the Eucharist in the early church was held in conjunction with a general meal. The problem in Corinth arose due to the social and economic differences among church members. The church was composed of both wealthy and poor, slaves and ex-slaves. Typically people would eat and drink what they brought to the gathering rather than sharing it with others in the way that we do at a potluck dinner. The wealthy, notes I. H. Marshall, "brought so much food and drink that they could indulge in gluttony and even in drunkenness. The poor, however, had little or nothing to bring, with the result that some of them went hungry and could not enjoy a decent meal. Paul further says that some people, presumably those who had more to eat, began eating before the others."[2]

Paul was clearly disturbed by this abuse of the Lord's Table and the way in which it violated the unity and love in the body of Christ, which the supper itself was designed to display (1 Cor. 10:17). This disregard for their poorer brethren, coupled with their riotous and even drunken behavior, constituted their sin. Selfishness and lack of love were the essence of their transgression, a fact that must be

---

[1] Ernest Kevan, *The Lord's Supper* (London: Evangelical Press, 1973), 23.
[2] I. Howard Marshall, *Last Supper and Lord's Supper* (Grand Rapids, MI: Eerdmans, 1980), 109.

kept in mind as we seek to make contemporary application of Paul's words.

We must also pay close attention to how closely the conclusion of verse 27 is related to the premise established in verses 23–26. These latter verses (27–32) state that the sacrament is designed to cultivate in us loving remembrance of all Christ accomplished on our behalf. At the Table we reflect on the nature and sufficiency of his death and thereby proclaim it to the world until he comes. Thus to partake in an unworthy manner is to do so without giving full consideration to the nature of the Supper as it is explained in verses 23–26. It is to partake with motives incompatible with the intent of Christ when he instituted the sacrament. It is to come to the Table with thoughts other than of his person and work. It is to come thinking of tomorrow's worries rather than Christ's return. It is to come remembering yesterday's disappointments rather than Christ's death. It is to partake in either ignorance of or conscious disregard for the instruction found in verses 23–26.

This sets the stage for Paul's statement concerning the consequences of unworthy participation: such a person "will be guilty concerning the body and blood of the Lord" (v. 27). Guilt is incurred when one profanes what is sacred by treating it as common. To despise the symbol is to despise that to which it points. If we abuse the Eucharist, we act with the calloused indifference and even malicious enmity of those who crucified him. Proper regard for the Lord's Supper is no small matter.

So how do we avoid partaking in an unworthy manner? In verse 28 Paul says we should "examine" ourselves. The word "examine" (Gk. *dokimadzo*) most often assumes the success of the test. It refers to the act of proving or testing something with a view to its emerging approved. The implication is that the self-examination will have a positive outcome. Either the individual will discover that he or she is already in a proper spiritual condition to receive the elements or will take the required steps to become so. Thus the point of self-examination is not to hinder participation but to make it possible and meaningful.

Also, to "examine" oneself entails analyzing one's understanding of the true meaning of the Eucharist. Why are we partaking? What do we hope to gain? Are we doing so in accordance with the purpose and spirit in which our Lord instituted the Supper? Is our partaking reverent? Is it a reflection of that unity in the body of Christ that Paul mentions in 1 Corinthians 10:17? To examine oneself is to ask these questions in preparation for approaching the Table in a spiritually appropriate frame of mind.

According to verse 29, the believer is to be careful about "discerning the body," or judging the body rightly. The word "body" may be a reference to the church, the body of believers. Indeed, in verses 17–22 the problem in Corinth is shown to be a failure to consider other members of the church. However, inasmuch as verse 29 is strikingly parallel to verse 27, I take "body" to be shorthand for the "body and blood" of the Lord himself. Therefore, not to discern the body rightly means not to perceive and reverence the Lord's Supper as a unique and sacred meal, thereby underestimating and devaluing its true character.

Paul speaks of *three distinct kinds of judgment* here.

There is first the judgment we apply to ourselves when we examine our hearts and test our motives to ensure that we partake in a way that honors Christ and the people of God.

Second, if we fail to judge ourselves in this way but persist in abusing the Lord's Table and profaning what is sacred, God will judge us physically by means of divine and fatherly discipline. This is not the loss of salvation. It is what God lovingly and graciously does to *prevent* the loss of salvation. This is precisely what had happened at Corinth. Those who in varying degrees had persisted in treating the Eucharist with contempt had, in varying degrees, come under divine discipline: some were weak physically, some were sick, and some had died.

Let's be careful here. Paul is not telling us that every time we become physically weak or exhausted and can't function well in life, it is because of some unrepentant sin in our lives. Nor is he saying that when we become ill or fall under an affliction of some sort, it is always because of sin in our lives. Don't interpret every head cold or arthritic knee or diagnosis of cancer as the discipline of God. Far less should we conclude that every time a Christian dies at an early age, it is divine discipline for unrepentant sin.

However, on occasion God does use physical affliction as a means to discipline us, to awaken us to our sin, and to draw us back to himself. And in the case of the Corinthians Paul declares that as a fact. He is speaking with apostolic authority based on what God had revealed to him: many in Corinth were under divine discipline for this particular sin; some even had died because of it. But we must be careful before we draw a direct, cause-and-effect connection between physical sickness and sin.

All this was to spare them the third kind of judgment—eternal and spiritual judgment. In verse 32 Paul speaks of this as being "condemned along with the world," that is to say, being subjected to the eternal judgment or condemnation that the non-Christian world will experience.

During the course of a personal conversation with John Piper, he said something about this passage that I found extremely challenging and helpful. I told him I was preaching a series on the subject of eternal security, and he informed me that the very next Sunday he was preaching on it as well. Our discussion turned to this passage in 1 Corinthians 11.

He said, "Sam, there's no way to avoid the fact that here we see that sometimes God will take the physical life of his own children in order to preserve and protect their spiritual life. Think about the implications of this. It seems to be that God foresees the natural trajectory of a person's life heading toward a pattern of sin that is incompatible with regeneration. He cuts them off before they get there and thus secures their eternal salvation."

In other words, one way that God "sustains" some of his people is by removing them from this life before they have opportunity to persist in their sin to such an extent that they apostatize.

I shot back at John: "But why would God do it this way?" After all, God can turn or incline our hearts toward good (see Prov. 21:1; 2 Thess. 3:5). So why doesn't he simply protect his people from such future sin by putting the fear of God in their hearts so that they will not turn from him (Jer. 32:40)? Why kill them to protect them?

God doesn't tell us why. Perhaps God allows it to happen in the lives of some of his children in order to show the rest of us the seriousness of our sin and disobedience. Perhaps he wants to demonstrate our utter dependence on him for life and holiness.

The other question, obviously, is this: If the born again are sometimes disciplined with physical death to keep them from being condemned with the world, does this mean the elect can lose their salvation?

The answer that both John and I gave, of course, was no. John added this: "It does confirm that there are patterns of sin which are finally incompatible with salvation. And God will take our lives rather than let us succumb to those patterns."

The point, then, is when our lives begin to move in a trajectory that is incompatible with our status as born-again children of God and that will end in eternal condemnation, on occasion God will intervene and turn us back. He will act upon our hearts by his Spirit to bring conviction of sin and eventually will turn us from this pathway to walk once again in righteousness. Praise God when he does it this way.

But on occasion God intervenes and takes the believer's life physically, precisely in order to preserve his life spiritually. That is what verse 32 is saying, as shocking as it may seem.

Of course, Paul is concerned with only one particular expression of unrepentant sin here in 1 Corinthians 11. Calloused disregard of the Lord's Table is only one example of the kinds of sin that call forth the loving discipline of our heavenly Father. And, yes, it *is* loving because, though painful, it is designed to restore us to the vibrancy of fellowship with Christ and, if necessary, to preserve us eternally safe in our salvation.

We could easily turn to Acts 5 and take note of a similar case, where Ananias and Sapphira are disciplined into heaven through premature physical death because of their lying to the Holy Spirit concerning the money they had pledged to the church in Jerusalem.

Now let me bring 1 Corinthians 1:8–9 into conjunction with 1 Corinthians 11:27–32. God has promised to preserve his people so that they will stand in his presence on the day when Jesus returns and be found guiltless. When we wander away from him and walk in disobedience, he most commonly does it by bringing conviction of sin to our hearts and working in us so that we will repent and turn back to him and gradually walk yet again in the way of holiness and obedience and love and purity. He preserves us in the security of our salvation by sustaining within us the faith that is absolutely essential to eternal life.

Another, less common, way in which God sustains one of his wayward children is by taking drastic steps to prevent him or her from walking down a path that leads to spiritual death. Physical death or temporal discipline thus on occasion becomes the means by which God ensures spiritual life in those who have been born again. That assuredly is what had occurred in the case of some in the church at Corinth in the first century.

2 CORINTHIANS 1:21–22

Yet another reason why I am so passionate about the reality of eternal security is the ministry of the Holy Spirit in our hearts. In 2 Corinthians 1 we are told that God has sealed us with his Spirit. As Paul said in Ephesians 1:13, "In him you also, when you heard the word of truth, the gospel of your salvation, and believed in him, were sealed with the promised Holy Spirit" (see also Eph. 4:30).

The term *seal*, when used literally, referred to a stamped impression in wax pointing to ownership and protection. When used metaphorically it meant (1) to authenticate (John 3:33; 6:27; 1 Cor. 9:2) or confirm as genuine and true (not unlike what happens when you take a document to be notarized), including the idea that what is sealed is stamped with the character of its owner; (2) to designate or mark out as one's property; to declare and signify ownership (see Rev. 7:3–8; 9:4); or (3) to render secure or to establish (i.e., protect; see Matt. 27:66; Eph. 4:30; Rev. 20:3).

All these texts (Eph. 1:13–14; 4:30; 2 Cor. 1:21–22) appear to suggest that the seal is the Spirit himself, "by whom God has marked believers and claimed them for his own."[3] In other words, it isn't so much that the Spirit does the sealing as that the Spirit *is* the seal (although it certainly could be both). Hence, sealing is nothing less than the reception and consequent indwelling of the Holy Spirit.

But Paul goes even further and declares that God has also "given us his Spirit in our hearts as a guarantee" (2 Cor. 1:22).

On three occasions Paul describes the Spirit as the down payment, the pledge, or the guarantee. The Greek term (*arrabon*) was used in commercial transactions to refer to the first installment of the total amount due. The down payment effectively guaranteed the fulfillment of whatever contractual obligations were assumed. "The Spirit, therefore," says Fee, "serves as God's down payment in our present lives, the certain evidence that the future has come into the present, the sure guarantee that the future will be realized in full measure."[4] This means that in giving the Holy Spirit to us, God does more than merely confirm our eternal inheritance; he also graciously provides a foretaste, if only in small measure, of what

---

[3] Gordon Fee, *God's Empowering Presence: The Holy Spirit in the Letters of Paul* (Peabody, MA: Hendrickson, 1994), 807.
[4] Ibid.

that inheritance will entail. In other words, when you become ex-perientially aware of the presence within of transcendent deity, of joy inexpressible and full of glory, of power that triumphs over the allure of fleshly lusts, of delight sweeter than the passing pleasures of sin, and of satisfaction that puts earthly success to shame, you are sensing, if only in small measure, what will be yours in infinite degree in the age to come.

It is nothing less than the precious Spirit of God quickening our soul to the reality of what awaits us on the other side, assuring us he is here, "in our hearts" (v. 22b), to guarantee that all God has promised will come to pass. We have it on no less authority than the Holy Spirit himself that what we sense in our spirit now is a divine guarantee and foretaste of what we will see and hear and feel and taste and enjoy throughout the ages to come in all the fullness of God himself.

But what about Psalm 51:11, where David cries out: "Cast me not away from your presence, and take not your Holy Spirit from me"? Doesn't this suggest the possibility that the Holy Spirit can be taken from us and that we can lose our salvation? No, I don't believe so.

Aside from the saving activity of the Holy Spirit in the Old Testa-ment and the empowering ministry by which believers were sancti-fied and enabled to live holy lives, the Holy Spirit was poured out in an extraordinary fashion on select individuals to equip them to perform important tasks in the covenant community of Israel:

1. Craftsmen who worked on the tabernacle (Ex. 31:1–6)
2. Civil administrators such as Moses and the seventy elders (Num. 11:16–17, 25–26)
3. Military commanders such as Joshua (Num. 27:18)
4. Judges appointed and empowered to rule over Israel (Judg. 3:10; 6:34)
5. Samson (Judg. 14:5–6, 19; 15:14; 16:20)
6. Prophets (1 Chron. 12:18; Mic. 3:8)

7. Kings over Israel, such as Saul (1 Sam. 10:1, 6, 10; 16:14) and David (1 Sam. 16:12–13)

Thus there was a ministry of the Holy Spirit in the Old Testament *unrelated to personal salvation*, designed solely to empower, enable, and equip someone for a task to which God had appointed him or her. This, I believe, is what David had in mind in Psalm 51:11. He prayed that God would not withdraw the anointing of the Spirit that empowered him to lead Israel as king. Indeed, he may well have had in mind that disturbing scene where "the Spirit of the LORD departed from Saul" (1 Sam. 16:14), praying that such would never befall him.

CONCLUSION

There will be times in the experience of every born-again Christian when God seems distant and uninvolved. There will be times when we struggle with doubt and fear and anxiety, times when we think our sin has put us beyond the reach of his forgiveness and grace. But if Jesus is our ultimate treasure, if our trust is in him alone, if we look to his life, death, and resurrection as our only hope, of this we may be certain: God will sustain us until the time of the end and present us guiltless in his presence. His Spirit has set a seal on our hearts, declaring loudly and clearly: you belong to God! His Spirit has taken up residence in our hearts, declaring loudly and clearly: your eternal inheritance is guaranteed!

Praise be to God for his glorious, preserving grace in our lives.

7

TEST YOURSELVES

If there is anything we can learn from this study on the subject of eternal security and apostasy, it is that we should avoid arrogant dogmatism. Although I am persuaded of the truth of eternal security and am quite passionate in my defense of it, I also recognize that certain biblical texts are problematic. Hebrews 6 is a case in point.[1] Yet once all the biblical evidence is weighed, the scales of balance incline heavily in favor of eternal security. At the same time, I do understand why some people struggle to embrace it.

Let's revisit our friend Charley for a moment as a way of setting the stage for an exploration of one of the most difficult passages in Scripture.

As a reminder, Charley was born into a Christian family, attended church throughout his teenaged years, and appeared to give every indication that he had put his faith in Jesus Christ. In college he fell in with a group of friends who challenged his faith and insisted he was naïve to believe in Jesus. Before long Charley stopped attending church, and eventually he declared himself an atheist. His anger and resentment toward anything remotely religious grew with each passing day. Charley is now thirty, twice divorced, an alcoholic, painfully bitter, and unpleasant to be around. He wants nothing ever again to do with Christianity. So what happened?

---

[1] Much of this chapter has been adapted from the treatment of Hebrews 6 in my book *Tough Topics: Biblical Answers to 25 Challenging Questions* (Wheaton, IL: Crossway, 2013). Used by permission of Crossway.

Those who insist that Charley was genuinely converted early in life but then apostatized and lost his salvation typically point to Hebrews 6 in defense of their view. In fact, many of you might have been asking, "Although Sam has made a good defense of eternal security, what about Hebrews 6:4–6? When is he going to tackle that thorny text?" Well, right now!

HEBREWS 6:4–6

It is impossible, in the case of those who have once been enlightened, who have tasted the heavenly gift, and have shared in the Holy Spirit, and have tasted the goodness of the word of God and the powers of the age to come, and then have fallen away, to restore them again to repentance, since they are crucifying once again the Son of God to their own harm and holding him up to contempt. (Heb. 6:4–6)

So, then, who are these people who fell away? It is important to know, because "it is impossible . . . to restore them again to repentance, since they are crucifying once again the Son of God to their own harm and holding him up to contempt."

There are probably a dozen or more interpretations of this passage.[2] I won't interact with them here; I want to focus solely on the question of whether the terminology in verses 4–5 would lead us to conclude that those who fell away were born-again believers.

If so, does that destroy the doctrine of eternal security? New Testament scholar and theological Calvinist Thomas Schreiner, who teaches at The Southern Baptist Theological Seminary in Louisville, Kentucky, doesn't think so. He believes these are indeed Christian men and women who are being warned about the eternal consequences of apostasy. The author of Hebrews doesn't assert that they *have* fallen away but admonishes them so that they won't. In other

---

[2] The best treatment of the more cogent options is found in Herbert W. Bateman IV, ed., *Four Views on the Warning Passages in Hebrews* (Grand Rapids, MI: Kregel, 2007).

words, the warnings are designed to awaken and empower and motivate Christians to escape the threatened consequence. The Lord uses such warnings as the means by which he prompts his people not to apostatize. None of God's elect, says Schreiner, will fail to heed the warning, and thus all will persevere. However, many find this unpersuasive and insist that if Christians cannot fall away from the faith, it is meaningless to warn them not to. But Schreiner directs our attention to Acts 27.

During the course of Paul's journey to Rome, a life-threatening storm erupted on the sea. Everyone's life was in danger, including that of Paul himself. In the middle of this storm Paul spoke to the crew on board:

> Since they had been without food for a long time, Paul stood up among them and said, "Men, you should have listened to me and not have set sail from Crete and incurred this injury and loss. Yet now I urge you to take heart, for *there will be no loss of life among you*, but only of the ship. For this very night there stood before me an angel of the God to whom I belong and whom I worship, and he said, 'Do not be afraid, Paul; you must stand before Caesar. And behold, God has granted you all those who sail with you.' So take heart, men, for I have faith in God that it will be exactly as I have been told." (Acts 27:21–25)

The divine promise is clear: no one will die as a result of the life-threatening weather. Nevertheless, a number of the sailors clearly didn't believe Paul and thus prepared a lifeboat in order to jump ship.

> And as the sailors were seeking to escape from the ship, and had lowered the ship's boat into the sea under pretense of laying out anchors from the bow, Paul said to the centurion and the soldiers, "Unless these men stay in the ship, you cannot be saved." Then the soldiers cut away the ropes of the ship's boat and let it go. (Acts 27:30–32)

Wait a minute! Didn't Paul say that God had promised no one would die? He did, but now he warns them that if they leave the ship, they will die. How does that work? Paul's warning is clear. Everyone was needed to direct the ship to safety. The apostle evidently did not think that the promise of survival precluded the need to warn them what would happen if they jumped ship. It seems the warning he issued was one of the means God employed to preserve all their lives. The warning is not emptied of significance simply because the threat of death never came to pass. The threat never came to pass because everyone heeded the warning. Schreiner then applies this principle to the many warning passages in Scripture, such as the one in Hebrews 6:

> The warnings to the elect are not meaningless simply because the threat never comes to pass for those who are truly saved. The elect escape the threatened judgment precisely by heeding the warning. And I would contend that all the elect heed the warning, and hence they never will face final judgment.[3]

Schreiner's point is well taken. However, I'm still not convinced that it applies to Hebrews 6.

This leads me to ask, Is it possible for a person to experience some form of spiritual enlightenment and to taste spiritual blessings and to partake of the Holy Spirit yet never know Jesus in a saving way? I believe the answer is yes (as we saw, for example, in our study of John's Gospel). Here are six reasons from the book of Hebrews itself why we can assume those people were *not* born-again believers who apostatized.

---

[3] Thomas R. Schreiner, *Run to Win the Prize: Perseverance in the New Testament* (Wheaton, IL: Crossway, 2010), 96. See also the much fuller treatment of this perspective in Thomas R. Schreiner and Ardel B. Caneday, *The Race Set before Us: A Biblical Theology of Perseverance and Assurance* (Downers Grove, IL: InterVarsity, 2001).

Reasons to Believe That the People in Hebrews 6:4–6 Were Not Christians[4]

First, the situation described in verses 4–6 is illustrated in verses 7–8. There we read, "For land that has drunk the rain that often falls on it [this drinking of frequent rain refers to the blessings of vv. 4–5: enlightenment, partaking of the Holy Spirit, tasting spiritual blessings, etc.], and produces a crop useful to those for whose sake it is cultivated, receives a blessing from God. But if it bears thorns and thistles [this corresponds to the "falling away" of v. 6a], it is worthless and near to being cursed, and its end is to be burned."

Rain falls on all kinds of ground, but one cannot tell from that alone what kind of vegetation, if any, will appear. The picture here is not of ground that receives frequent rain, yields life and vegetation, and then loses it. The picture is of two different kinds of ground. One responds to the rain [spiritual blessings and opportunities] by producing bountiful vegetation, while the other is barren, lifeless, and thus condemned. Likewise, people who hear the gospel and respond with saving faith bring forth life. Others, however, who sit in church and hear the truth and are blessed by the ministry of the Holy Spirit but eventually turn their back on it all are like a field that never yields vegetation and thus come into judgment.

Second, in 6:9 we read of a significant contrast: "Though we speak in this way, yet in your case, beloved, we feel sure of better things—things that belong to salvation." The "better things" in view are stated in verses 10–12 and include work, love, serving the saints, diligence, full assurance of hope, faith, patience, and inheriting the promises. These "things" are "better" than the experiences of verses 4–6 precisely because they "belong to" salvation.

In other words, the author of Hebrews is confident that most of those reading his letter have experienced and displayed "better

[4] The best treatment of the view I defend here is provided by Wayne Grudem, "Perseverance of the Saints: A Case Study from the Warning Passages in Hebrews," in *Still Sovereign: Contemporary Perspectives on Election, Foreknowledge, and Grace*, ed. Thomas R. Schreiner and Bruce A. Ware (Grand Rapids, MI: Baker, 2000), 133–82.

things" than those whom he describes in verses 4–6. These things are better because they involve salvation. His obvious point is that the blessings in verses 4–6 do *not* pertain to salvation. The contrast is clear.

Before going further, let's summarize verses 7–12. The illustration in verses 7–8 compares the people in verses 4–6 to land that fails to produce fruit. It yields only thorns and thistles. These people, then, were obviously never genuinely converted. Then, in verses 9–12, he says that his readers, whom he calls "beloved" (v. 9a), have experienced "better things" than any of the temporary experiences of verses 4–6. These are "things" that pertain to the genuine experience of salvation. It would seem clear, then, that both the analogy in verses 7–8 and the explicit assertion in verse 9 tell us that the people described in verses 4–6 were never truly saved in the first place.

Third, according to Hebrews 3:14 (and 3:6), "we have come to share in Christ, if indeed we hold our original confidence firm to the end." As we saw earlier, he says we *"have come"* to share in Christ, not "will come" or "are now partakers," if we persevere in faith. In other words, holding fast in faith—persevering and producing spiritual fruit—proves that you *became* a partaker of Christ in the past. Failing to hold fast or apostatizing from the faith proves that you *never were* a partaker of Christ. Apostasy or falling away (6:6a) doesn't mean you once were in and have now fallen out of a saving relationship to Christ. It means you never were with Christ in the first place.

Fourth, we read in Hebrews 10:14 that "by a single offering he has perfected for all time those who are being sanctified." Here we are told that for those who are now being sanctified (i.e., indwelt by the Holy Spirit, growing in holiness by faith) "the offering of Christ on the cross *has perfected that person for all time*. For all time! In other words to become a beneficiary of the perfecting, justifying work of Christ on the cross is to be perfected in the sight of God forever. This suggests that Hebrews 6:6 does not mean that those who re-crucify

Christ were once really justified by the blood of Jesus and were really being sanctified in an inward spiritual sense."[5]

Fifth, our author concludes this letter with a prayer relating to the fulfillment in us of the blessings of the new covenant. He prays that God would "equip you with everything good that you may do his will, working in us that which is pleasing in his sight, through Jesus Christ, to whom be glory forever and ever. Amen" (Heb. 13:21). This is the promise of the new and "eternal" covenant (v. 20), that God will put in his people a new heart and cause them to walk in his ways and not turn away from doing them good (see Jer. 24:7; 32:40; Ezek. 11:19; 36:27).

This prayer clearly tells us that perseverance in faith and in doing God's will is ultimately the work of God in us. It is finally dependent not on us but on God. This is the way he fulfills his promise in the new covenant. But if some of God's people fail to remain believers and to pursue holiness of life and thus apostatize from the faith, God will himself have failed to fulfill his promise to work in us what "is pleasing in his sight."

Sixth, we must take note not just of what is said but of what is *not* said of these people in verses 4–6.[6] Typical terms used to describe believers such as *regeneration, conversion, justified, adopted, elect*, and *faith in Jesus* are conspicuously absent. This is more than merely an argument from silence when we consider the way Christians are described in the book of Hebrews itself. Here is a listing of what is said in Hebrews of the true believer, all of which is absent from the description of those who apostatize in 6:4–6.

1. God has forgiven their sins (10:17; 8:12)
2. God has cleansed their consciences (9:14; 10:22)
3. God has written his laws on their hearts (8:10; 10:16)
4. God is producing holiness of life in them (2:11; 10:14; 13:21)

[5] John Piper, "When Is Saving Repentance Impossible?," sermon, October 13, 1996, http://www.desiring god.org. I've been greatly helped by Piper's insights on Hebrews 6.
[6] See Grudem, "Perseverance," 162–68.

5. God has given them an unshakable kingdom (12:28)
6. God is pleased with them (11; 13:16, 21)
7. They have faith (4:3; 6:12; 10:22, 38, 39; 12:2; 13:7; etc.)
8. They have hope (6:11, 18; 7:19; 10:23)
9. They have love (6:10; 10:33–34; 13:1)
10. They worship and pray (12:28; 13:15; 4:16; 10:22)
11. They obey God (5:9; 10:36; 12:10, 11, 14)
12. They persevere (3:6, 14; 6:11; 10:23)
13. They enter God's rest (4:3, 11)
14. They know God (8:11)
15. They are God's house, his children, his people
    (3:6; 2:10, 13; 8:10)
16. They share in Christ (3:14)
17. They will receive future salvation (1:14; 5:9; 7:25; 9:28)

Someone might object, "Okay, typical descriptions of the saved are not found in 6:4–6, but neither are typical descriptions of the lost found there." That's true. But that is to be expected. After all, before they commit apostasy, their spiritual status is uncertain. No one can know with certainty whether they are truly saved. "It remains to be seen whether they are among the saved or the lost. They have not yet given decisive indications either way. That is the reason the author warns them not to turn away—they are still at a point where a decision to be among the saved or the lost must be made."[7]

How Can Non-Christians Be Described in These Terms?

What about the terms used in 6:4–5 (enlightened, tasted, shared, etc.)? On the one hand, it is certainly the case that all Christians experience these realities. But do *only* Christians experience them? Is it possible that they can also be experienced by people who have been repeatedly exposed to the gospel and the benefits it brings,

7 Ibid., 171.

even when they haven't personally embraced the person of Christ as Lord and Savior? Let's look at each one in turn.

1) They have "once been enlightened" (v. 4). "Enlightened" need mean no more than to hear the gospel, to learn or to understand. Countless non-Christians grew up in church and perhaps attended a Christian college or seminary and therefore understand a great deal about the Christian faith. The Holy Spirit can actually enlighten them and give them insight, which they in turn ultimately reject. Merely understanding Christian doctrines does not prove one is saved. All of us know people, perhaps family members, who have been repeatedly exposed to the truth of the gospel, understand what it means, can articulate the claims of Christ with incredible precision, yet refuse to put their trust in him as Lord and Savior. Thus, whereas all true Christians have been enlightened, not all those who are enlightened are true Christians.

2) They have "tasted the heavenly gift" (v. 4) and "the goodness of the word of God" and "the powers of the age to come" (v. 5). This certainly points to a genuine spiritual experience. But must we conclude that it was a genuine *saving* experience? They are not strangers to the gospel or to the church and have come under conviction of the Holy Spirit. They have experienced some degree of blessing, both through common grace and through their close, intimate contact with genuine believers.

Perhaps they have been healed (the vast majority whom Jesus healed were not saved). Perhaps a demon has been cast out. They have heard the Word of God and have come to taste and feel and enjoy something of its power and beauty and truth. They have felt the wooing of the Spirit and have seen wonderful things in the body of Christ. Those in Matthew 7:22–23 preached, prophesied, performed miracles, and cast out demons in Christ's name, but they were not saved. Jesus said to them: "I never knew you; depart from me, you workers of lawlessness" (v. 23). These, then, "have tasted" the power and blessings of the new covenant, but they have not personally prized, cherished, embraced, loved, trusted, treasured, or savored the atoning death of Jesus as their only hope for eternal life.

3) They "have shared in the Holy Spirit" (v. 4). Whereas the word translated "shared" or "partaken" can certainly refer to a saving participation in Christ (cf. Heb. 3:14), it can also refer to a looser association or participation (see Luke 5:7; Heb. 1:9, "companions"). These people had in some way come to share in some aspect of the Holy Spirit and his ministry, but must we conclude that it was a saving way? Why does our author *not* use terminology that would put the question of their spiritual status to rest, such as "filled with" the Spirit or "baptized in" or "indwelt by" the Holy Spirit?

4) They have in some sense repented (v. 6). There is a sorrow for sins and a turning from them that even nonbelievers can experience. This is clear from Hebrews 12:17 and the reference to Esau, as well as the "repentance" of Judas Iscariot in Matthew 27:3. Paul refers to a repentance "that leads to salvation without regret" (2 Cor. 7:10a) as well as a "worldly grief [that] produces death" (2 Cor. 7:10b). The implication is that there is a repentance that does *not* lead to salvation. As with belief and faith, so too with repentance—we must always distinguish between what is substantial and saving and what is spurious.

Wayne Grudem provides this helpful summation:

What has happened to these people? They are at least people who have been affiliated closely with the fellowship of the church. They have had some sorrow for sin and a decision to forsake their sin (*repentance*). They have clearly understood the gospel and given some assent to it (they have been *enlightened*). They have come to appreciate the attractiveness of the Christian life and the change that comes about in people's lives because of becoming a Christian, and they have probably had answers to prayers in their own lives and felt the power of the Holy Spirit at work, perhaps even using some spiritual gifts (they have become "associated with" the work of the Holy

Spirit or have become *partakers* of the Holy Spirit and have tasted the heavenly gift and the powers of the age to come).

They have been exposed to the true preaching of the Word and have appreciated much of its teachings (they have *tasted* the goodness of the Word of God). These factors are all positive, and people who have experienced these things may be genuine Christians. But these factors alone are not enough to give conclusive evidence of any of the decisive beginning stages of the Christian life (regeneration, saving faith and repentance unto life, justification, adoption, initial sanctification). In fact, *these experiences are all preliminary to those decisive beginning stages of the Christian life.* The actual spiritual status of those who have experienced these things is still unclear.[8]

I conclude that the people described in 6:4–5 who, according to verse 6, "have fallen away" are not now and never were born-again believers. They are not Christians who lost their salvation. They are non-Christians who perhaps made a profession of faith in Jesus, were baptized in water, perhaps became members of a church and even participated in leadership, and then willfully and with a hard heart turned away and rejected everything they had come to know.

The spiritual state and experience of those described in Hebrews 6:4–6 is virtually identical to that of the first three of four soils in the parable of the sower (see Matt. 13:3–23; Mark 4:1–9; Luke 8:4–15). In that parable, only the fourth soil is called "good" and subsequently bears fruit. The other three represent those who hear the gospel and respond with varying degrees of understanding, interest, and joy, none of which, however, bears fruit that would testify of genuine spiritual life. They experienced "enlightenment" and "tasted" the goodness and power of the ministry of the Spirit and the blessings of the kingdom yet turned their back on the truth when trials, troubles,

---

[8] Ibid., 153 (emphasis original).

or temptations came their way. Their apostasy was proof of the falsity of their initial faith (see esp. John 8:31; Heb. 3:6, 14; 1 John 2:19).

My response to the Hebrews 6 passage, therefore, isn't to lament over those who once were saved but now are irrevocably lost. My response is to appeal to you who have become comfortable in your surface familiarity with the Christian faith yet have kept Christ at arm's length. My appeal is to you who have grown in your understanding of Christianity and have experienced great blessings because of your presence in and association with the church, yet you do not trust and treasure Jesus above all else. I appeal to you to repent and believe the gospel, lest after some time you fall away from what you know and are guilty of holding Christ up for contempt.

Finally, it is impossible to restore them to repentance not because God lacks the power to do so. Rather, it is because God *refuses* to do so. To those who have experienced such blessings and have come so close to genuine conversion, only to willfully turn their backs on Jesus and thus, in effect, reenact the public shame of his crucifixion and subject him to open contempt, God says, "Have it your way. I release you to pursue your chosen path. That you experienced such gracious gifts and came so close, only to spit in the face of Jesus Christ, is so wicked and hard-hearted that I will no longer deal with you."

Some who embrace the doctrine of eternal security hold to the belief "once saved, always saved." But if you believe that born-again Christians can apostatize and lose their salvation, you must embrace the doctrine of "twice lost, always lost." In other words, they were lost; then they were saved, only to apostatize and find themselves irreversibly lost, because Hebrews 6 says it is impossible to renew them to repentance.

I believe Hebrews 6 is saying that there are some among those not born again who, in spite of having experienced great and glorious blessings from the Holy Spirit and in spite of their exposure to the gospel, have come so very close to true conversion but then have hardened their hearts to such a degree that when they finally and fully turn away from Christ, God simply lets them go.

2 CORINTHIANS 13:5

Let's close by meditating for a moment on what Paul says in 2 Corinthians 13:5.[9] Most often people who live in fear that they aren't saved are the ones who need worry about it the least. Unregenerate people couldn't care less about their sin or salvation. They find the beauty of Christ unattractive and are indifferent toward the countless ways in which they violate his will and fail to honor him as God.

If you are painfully concerned over your sin and distressed by your failure to love and obey Christ as you know you should, I feel free to encourage you and reassure your heart that you do, indeed, truly know him as Lord and Savior. It is the stinging conviction of sin that testifies to the Spirit's saving presence in your heart.

There are many saved who think they aren't but an even greater number who aren't saved but think they are. They are the ones who need to hear Hebrews 6. Many who walked an aisle when they were seven or prayed a prayer at the age of twelve or assume that living in the United States and being raised in a church necessarily entails salvation presumptuously believe themselves to be Christians whose eternal destiny is set and secure.

D. A. Carson has articulated what we know all too well, that "there are millions of professing believers in North America today (to say nothing of elsewhere) who at some point entered into a shallow commitment to Christianity, but who, if pushed, would be forced to admit they do not love holiness, do not pray, do not hate sin, do not walk humbly with God. They stand in the same danger as the Corinthians; and Paul's warning applies to them no less than to the Corinthian readers of this epistle."[10]

---

[9] For a more complete explanation of this passage, see my book *A Sincere and Pure Devotion to Christ: 100 Daily Meditations on 2 Corinthians*, vol. 2 (Wheaton, IL: Crossway, 2010), 259–63.
[10] D. A. Carson, *From Triumphalism to Maturity: An Exposition of 2 Corinthians 10–13* (Grand Rapids, MI: Baker, 1984), 178.

Here in 2 Corinthians 13:5 we find the apostle Paul issuing a pointed and passionate call to the Corinthian church. "Examine yourselves," says Paul, "to see whether you are in the faith. Test yourselves. Or do you not realize this about yourselves, that Jesus Christ is in you?—unless indeed you fail to meet the test!"

To fail the test is to discover, after self-examination, that Jesus is not in them. Paul is not talking about a true Christian apostatizing and then discovering that Jesus is no longer there. His point is that if the Corinthians are truly Christians, they will realize that Jesus *is* in them.

Certainly Paul believed that the majority of those in Corinth were true believers (see 3:1–3; 6:13). However, although they are confident that they will "pass the test," the possibility exists that some may discover they have failed. In other words, the reality of self-delusion and false assurance must be faced.

This is where we must turn our focus from the first century to the twenty-first, from the Corinthians and their spiritual state to us and ours. How should we today examine ourselves?

Perhaps we should begin where Paul did, with the objective, re-velatory truths found in God's Word—"the faith" (v. 5), as he put it. Are we in it? Are our beliefs governed by Scripture or by personal likes and dislikes? Do we elevate our opinions above God's? Most important of all, who is Jesus to us? Do we accept Scripture's claim that he is God incarnate, that he lived a sinless life and died a substitutionary death, absorbing in himself the wrath of God we deserve, and that he rose again bodily from the dead? Do we set our hope in our sincerity and the confidence that our good deeds will somehow trump our bad ones?

What is our response to the apostolic message? Does it resonate in our heart? Do we relish the revelation of Christ about whom Paul and Peter and John and others wrote and for whose name's sake they gave their lives? Are we submissive to their teaching? Do we shape our lives, recast our beliefs, and formulate our choices to conform with the theological and ethical principles they defend?

We must also examine ourselves by determining not whether we sin, because we most certainly do, but how we feel and respond when we sin. Are we indifferent and cold toward our failures? Do we find ways to rationalize what we know is inconsistent with Scripture? Do we simply acquiesce to our sinful desires and lusts, saying, "That's how God made me, so it can't be wrong. I'm just being me. Surely God can't argue with that."

I certainly don't want to endorse a morbid, introspective obsession with the state of our souls, as if we are called upon each moment to take our spiritual pulse, oblivious to the hurts and needs and desperate condition of those around us. But we must also avoid the opposite extreme that is characterized by presumptuous self-delusion and a proud indifference to the ethical demands of the gospel.

In conclusion, and most important, when we realize that nothing in our life is perfect, that all our beliefs are to some extent flawed, and that every effort we make is tainted by selfishness and sin, do we look to Jesus alone, whose life, death, and resurrection are our only hope? That is the ultimate test.

8

WHATEVER GOD STARTS, HE FINISHES

I was blessed in my days at the University of Oklahoma to have a spiritual mentor who cared deeply for my growth and wasn't afraid to speak hard truth when I needed to hear it. He was especially fond of saying three things. First, "Those whom God chooses, he changes." Second, "Whatever God requires, he provides." And third, "Whatever God starts, he finishes." It is the third of these that I want us to consider as we turn our attention to several more of Paul's statements.

1 THESSALONIANS 5:23–24 AND 2 THESSALONIANS 3:1–5

Among the many passages where we find the apostle's emphasis on God's faithfulness to sustain and preserve his people, two are in Paul's correspondence to the Thessalonians:

> Now may the God of peace himself sanctify you completely, and may your whole spirit and soul and body be kept blameless at the coming of our Lord Jesus Christ. *He who calls you is faithful; he will surely do it.*" (1 Thess. 5:23–24)

> Finally, brothers, pray for us, that the word of the Lord may speed ahead and be honored, as happened among you, and that we may be delivered from wicked and evil men. For not

all have faith. *But the Lord is faithful. He will establish you and guard you against the evil one.* And we have confidence in the Lord about you, that you are doing and will do the things that we command. May the Lord direct your hearts to the love of God and to the steadfastness of Christ. (2 Thess. 3:1–5)

A frequent response to these texts goes something like this: "What if Paul actually meant to say that God will sustain us until the coming of Christ Jesus *only if* we continue in faith and love and obedience to him? What if God's commitment to sanctify us completely and guard us against the attack of Satan is conditional and thus hangs on whether we first choose to remain faithful to him?" I have two responses.

First, that's not what these texts say. Don't read into a passage something that's not there simply because you are afraid or because you don't like what *is* there. Second, and more important still, those who voice this concern are obviously worried about whether they will persevere in faith and holiness. But Paul asserts in these and similar texts that this is precisely what the faithful God has committed to do on behalf of his children. God has committed to do everything necessary to ensure that we will continue in faith, love, and obedience.

In other words, Paul asserts the very thing that some deny—God's people will persevere. They will not apostatize because God is faithful to sustain and establish his own in their relationship with Jesus until Jesus comes back. What does it mean for God to "sustain" us if not that God will keep us in our faith, preserve us in obedience, and do whatever is necessary to ensure that we will not apostatize or be cut off from his love?

The fear that grips the hearts of many is whether they will continue on the path of sanctification or progressive conformity with Christ. After all, we've seen repeatedly that the failure to do so is an indication that one most likely was never born again in the first place. "How can I be certain that what I've only started will in fact be brought to completion? How can I know in a way that will bring peace and joy to my heart that on the day of Christ Jesus my whole spirit and soul and body will be kept blameless? What assurances do I have that Satan will not destroy my faith or lead me into the depths of sin and apostasy?"

The answer isn't, "Ah, don't worry. Since you are eternally secure, it ultimately doesn't matter how far from the path of righteousness you might stray. Your sin, perhaps even your apostasy, doesn't have any ultimate effect on your eternal destiny. Remember: once saved, always saved!" No, that's not the answer. The biblical response is first to embrace the necessity of obedience, progressive growth in holiness, and steadfast faith in Jesus. Then, second, to rejoice in the assurances from God himself that he will remain faithful to his children precisely by exerting sufficient influence on their hearts that faith never dies, that holiness is still alive, and that perseverance is not merely a hope but a living reality.

If we must first remain faithful, only after which God promises to be faithful on our behalf, why need he bother at all? That is to say, if we are not only responsible but ultimately capable of keeping ourselves in faith and obedience without God's faithful presence to preserve us there, his action is rendered moot. There is no need for the promise of divine faithfulness if human faithfulness will get us by. We must never forget that the faithfulness required of us—and make no mistake: it *is* required—is precisely what God is faithful to provide. Yes, we do have to remain faithful to persevere. And, yes, the power and incentive to do so is what God pledges to produce in us and through us. Gordon Fee is on the mark in this regard:

> For the Thessalonians this is the needed reminder that neither their "sanctification" nor their being "preserved blameless" for the Parousia is dependent on their own personal struggling for it, but on their trusting the God who has already called them to

himself, and who will thus bring to pass in their lives what God has begun. In the end everything depends on the single reality that God is absolutely faithful.[1]

God doesn't merely call his people to sanctification or point them in the direction they should go. He faithfully supplies every need, all the power, every incentive, and whatever spiritual resolve is needed so that each of us who knows Jesus truly will finally stand in his presence blameless and whole.

PHILIPPIANS 1:6

Paul spoke with just as much energy and confidence when he declared:

> And I am sure of this, that he who began a good work in you will bring it to completion at the day of Jesus Christ. (Phil. 1:6)

Yes, whatever God starts, he finishes! That is Paul's point in Philippians 1:6. The "good work" initiated in the hearts of the Philippian believers will not fall short of the final goal. The new birth, wrought in them through the Holy Spirit, will not suffer interruption and fail to produce the good works and obedience that testify to the reality of what they claim. God promises that he "will bring it to completion at the day of Jesus Christ," which means that whatever is required along the pathway of our Christian lives, whatever faith is needed, whatever obedience is required, whatever repentance is called for, and whatever endurance we must display, God will work in us through his Spirit so that we will stand before his presence, wholly sanctified in body, soul, and spirit, blameless and without reproach. I am as sure of this as Paul is: "And *I am sure of this,* that he who began a good work in you will bring it to completion at the

[1] Gordon D. Fee, *The First and Second Letters to the Thessalonians*, The New International Commentary on the New Testament (Grand Rapids, MI: Eerdmans, 2009), 231.

day of Jesus Christ" (the italics are mine but the spiritual emphasis is Paul's).

Paul had seen his fair share of people who loudly proclaimed their faith in Jesus only later to betray that they never truly knew him as Lord and Savior. But he is confident beyond all doubt that what God had started in the lives of the Philippians, he would in fact finish. That isn't to say that they wouldn't face obstacles or that Satan had given up trying to deceive them and derail their faith. It isn't to say that the Philippians had graduated into some super-spiritual condition that put them beyond the reach of temptation and sin.

Neither is Paul suggesting that they need not strive to maintain their spiritual diligence and pursue holiness. He is saying that God is faithful to his work. God will do whatever it takes to uphold the Philippians in their faith in Jesus, and you in your faith in Jesus. God will persevere in his commitment to supply us with whatever it takes so that our confidence in Christ will not fail or falter, and the work of grace he began will ultimately be brought to its proper goal when Jesus returns.

Some of you are saying to yourselves even now: "This promise is only true for those who don't walk away from their faith in Jesus Christ." But that is to misunderstand what Paul is saying. He is confident that *God won't let you walk away*. If God wasn't committed to finishing the work of salvation he began, we would all walk away and apostatize. But we won't, because God will do everything necessary to bring us safely into his presence all the way to the end.

The assurance that fills Paul's heart and accounts in part for the joy that floods his prayers on their behalf is that God will do whatever it takes to guarantee that no born-again child of God will ever lapse into unbelief and apostasy. That isn't to say that the people of God won't at times spiritually drift and even fall into a backslidden and bitter state of soul. But their heavenly Father will never let them fail so as to fall completely out of his loving arms.

Take this text right now and impress its truth on your heart. I'm thinking particularly of those of you who are struggling with doubts about where you stand with God. You're plagued by fear and anxiety that God has given up on you. He's quite simply had enough; he's had his fill of you and your pathetic efforts to remain true to him. Listen to me. No, listen to *God* speaking to you through Paul. *Whatever God starts, he finishes.* I pray this truth will echo repeatedly in your mind and spirit so that you will be energized to get back in the race and resume the battle with the world, the flesh, and the Devil, renewed with the confident assurance that they can't win.

This passage and so many like it is why I have repeated that the reason why Christians persevere in their faith is that God preserves them in it. God will not give up on the elect; he will not abandon them with the job only half done; he will not permit any obstacle or opposition to stand in the way of bringing all his children into the full inheritance of what he has promised in Jesus.

1 Peter 1:1–5

The faithfulness of God in preserving his people through faith is nowhere better stated than by Peter in his first epistle:[2]

> Peter, an apostle of Jesus Christ, To those who are elect exiles of the Dispersion in Pontus, Galatia, Cappadocia, Asia, and Bithynia, according to the foreknowledge of God the Father, in the sanctification of the Spirit, for obedience to Jesus Christ and for sprinkling with his blood: May grace and peace be multiplied to you. Blessed be the God and Father of our Lord Jesus Christ! According to his great mercy, he has caused us to be born again to a living hope through the resurrection of Jesus Christ from the dead, to an inheritance that is imperishable, undefiled, and unfading, kept in heaven for you, who by God's

---

[2] In understanding this passage I was greatly helped by John Piper's sermon, "The Elect Are Kept by the Power of God," October 17, 1993, http://www.desiringgod.org. I have drawn extensively from Piper's comments.

power are being guarded through faith for a salvation ready to be revealed in the last time. (1 Pet. 1:1–5)

Here Peter describes our salvation as if it were a chain with several interlocking links. The first link in Peter's chain of salvation is election according to the foreknowledge of God (v. 1). The second link is the work of the Spirit in calling and consecrating the believer as God's own possession. The next link is our obedience to Jesus, first in trusting him for our salvation and then, of course, living in obedience to him throughout the course of our earthly lives. The final link in Peter's chain is inheriting on that final day the fullness of salvation.

But what if some link in the chain should break? What if there is a disruption in God's purpose such that one of his elect fails to stay faithful to Jesus? According to Peter, the reason we know that the chain will never come unlinked is that God is protecting us by his infinite power through faith until that final day. So Peter portrays the Christian as elect, set apart for God, and living in faith in Jesus. You've experienced the new birth and are given a living hope. But your salvation isn't complete. There is an inheritance yet to come, waiting for you in heaven. But what guarantee is there, if any, that you will still be standing on that day to inherit what God has promised? After all, as we've already noted, there are incredible dangers along the way that threaten to undo us, to destroy us, to lead us into unbelief and apostasy and death. What assurances do we have that we will be kept safe and secure and protected until that day?

Our protection comes from God. More specifically, it comes from the *power* of God. Our security doesn't mean that there is no battle or that we don't have to win it; it means that God will fight for us with infallible skill and omnipotent power. And the means God uses to protect us is *faith*. "[We] are [now] being guarded through faith."

Now ask yourself this: What is God guarding or protecting us from? What is it that threatens to sever the chain of salvation?

I doubt if Peter had physical death in mind, for when we die, we go immediately into the presence of God. The many ways in which we might suffer, whether physically, mentally, or emotionally, are also excluded, because Peter tells us in verses 6–7 that suffering serves to refine and purify our faith. Perhaps it's Satan from whom we need protection. Or perhaps it's the many temptations we face each day to abandon God and turn our back on Jesus. But these and every other kind of attack would succeed *only if we fell into unbelief*, only if we ceased to trust God, only if we failed to continue in faith in Christ who loved us and gave himself for us.

There is something of a paradox here in verse 5. On the one hand, it seems as if it is precisely our "faith" that puts us in spiritual jeopardy. All of us are keenly aware of the many ways our faith is challenged and assaulted. It weakens and wanes, and at times we feel as if we've lost it altogether. We doubt God's goodness. We question his decisions. We wonder if he is present. We accuse him of not loving us. We can't figure out why he let a loved one die so early in life. We can't figure out why he let a despicable degenerate live so long. The trials we face and the hardships and the temptations of the world, the flesh, and the Devil all conspire to lead us to renounce our faith.

On the other hand, Peter says it is precisely *through* our faith that God keeps us secure. Through our faith we are preserved and protected for that final day when the inheritance he has promised will be ours. The picture is that of a military fortress or camp inside of which are the elect exiles. Outside, the forces of evil launch relentless assaults. But surrounding the fortress is the power of God. The elect are preserved simply by putting their hope and trust in what God has said he will do for them.

God provides protection not from suffering or trials but from the possibility of falling away because of them. The faith under attack is the faith that in verse 7 is refined by trials. Obtaining our final inheritance does not bypass us, as if we had no part or responsibility.

The elect must continue to exercise faith, not simply that initial act of trusting Christ but the ongoing, daily trust in God.

But if experiencing that final salvation is dependent on our persevering faith, is it possible that some of those who were "elect according to the foreknowledge of God" might fail to attain it? Is it possible that some who were "sanctified" or set apart for God by the Spirit might come short of that faith, which is required for final salvation? Is it possible that some who were chosen and set apart for obedience to Jesus might fail to "obey" him in that they cease to have faith and thus fall short of inheriting that final salvation?

No! It is precisely God's power in the service of God's purpose that sustains God's people in their faith in him. God's power protects us from unbelief. The fact that God's purpose is to put his power at work on behalf of his people to guard them for the final salvation does not mean we can respond by saying, "If God's power is protecting me, I can live however I please. I can indulge in sin and enjoy the world and not worry about losing my salvation, because God's power is at work to keep me safe."

It means that God's power protects us for salvation precisely by sustaining our faith. The only thing that can keep us from heaven is forsaking our faith in Christ and turning to other hopes, other treasures. So to protect us, God prevents that. He inspires, nourishes, strengthens, and builds our faith, and in so doing he secures us against the only thing that could destroy us: unbelief.

This truth was surely especially precious to Peter. On the night when he betrayed Jesus, the Lord said to him, "Simon, Simon, behold, Satan demanded to have you, that he might sift you like wheat, but I have prayed for you that your faith may not fail. And when you have turned again, strengthen your brothers" (Luke 22:31–32). The reason why Peter wept bitterly following his betrayal of Jesus and why his faith did not entirely disappear is that Jesus prayed that he would stand firm in his belief. Jesus interceded with the Father on Peter's behalf: "Do not let Peter's faith fail. Sustain him by the Spirit. Don't let his confidence in me disappear" (of course, I'm only speculating on what Jesus might have prayed, but pray he did). Thus it was God, as Peter himself would later write, who guarded his apostle through faith, notwithstanding how very close he came to stumbling so as to fall. Peter's tears of repentance were a gift of God designed to keep him secure in the salvation that Christ died to obtain.

Clearly Peter knew from personal experience what he was talking about. Those, such as the apostle, who are born again unto a living hope are "guarded through faith for a salvation ready to be revealed in the last time." God is not only the author of the new birth and the one who imparts faith as a gift to his elect; he is also the sustaining power in their souls by which they remain finally faithful to him. He caused us to be born again by creating our faith, and he protects us on the way to heaven by preserving our faith.

JUDE 24–25

Jude, "a servant of Jesus Christ and brother of James" (Jude 1a), addressed his short letter "to those who are called, beloved in God the Father and kept for Jesus Christ" (v. 1b). In bringing his letter to a close, he virtually exploded in a burst of unbridled praise:

> Now to him who is able to keep you from stumbling and to present you blameless before the presence of his glory with great joy, to the only God, our Savior, through Jesus Christ our Lord, be glory, majesty, dominion, and authority, before all time and now and forever. Amen. (vv. 24–25)

If a genuine believer could fully and finally fall from saving grace and fail to enter into the inheritance of eternal life, God the Father would not be deserving of our ascription of glory or our heartfelt praise. Here in Jude, God is deemed worthy of adoration precisely because he "is able to keep you."

God is keenly aware of the perils and pitfalls that his people face in trying to remain faithful in this world. He knows how difficult spiritual fidelity can be. He is not ignorant of what you face, whether temptations or trials. He sees and knows the power of the world and its allure, its appeal, and the power of its promises. He is cognizant of every stone over which you might stumble, every cliff off which you might fall, and every dark alley down which you may wander. And he is more than able to keep you safe in the midst of it all.

The background to Jude's language may well come from numerous instances in the Psalms where God is portrayed as delivering his people from stumbling: "You have delivered my soul from death, yes, my feet from falling, that I may walk before God in the light of life" (56:13); "You have delivered my soul from death, my eyes from tears, my feet from stumbling" (116:8). Psalm 121:3–8 is especially relevant:

> He will not let your foot be moved;
>> he who keeps you will not slumber.
> Behold, he who keeps Israel
>> will neither slumber nor sleep.
> The Lord is your keeper;
>> the Lord is your shade on your right hand.
> The sun shall not strike you by day,
>> nor the moon by night.
> The Lord will keep you from all evil;
>> he will keep your life.
> The Lord will keep
>> your going out and your coming in
>> from this time forth and forevermore.

To properly understand the word "keep" (which is more literally translated "guard"), we must again note 2 Thessalonians 3:3: "The Lord is faithful. He will establish you and *guard* you against the evil one." This is an issue of God's faithfulness as much as his power. It's a matter of character. His integrity is at stake in his guarding of you. If he were to lose so much as one blood-bought child, both his faithfulness and his power would be suspect (see also John 17:11, 15; 1 Pet. 1:5). The fact that we don't stumble isn't because we are especially noble or strong or committed, but because God is. Left to ourselves, we are hopeless and helpless.

We do have a responsibility to keep ourselves, as Jude 21 makes clear: "Keep yourselves in the love of God." The promise of verse 24 does not cancel out the command of verse 21. Rather, verse 24 is the explanation of how we do it. God keeps us and empowers us to fulfill the command he issues (see Phil. 2:12–13; Heb. 13:20–21).

Jude 24–25 isn't a promise of sinless perfection but an assurance that God will never permit us to apostatize or fail to attain that eternal and joyful standing in his presence. Jude's emphasis is less on the ability of the saint to persevere than on the ability of God to preserve. Yes, we must remain committed to him, and we shall remain committed because he remains committed to us.

Okay, you say, I'll concede the fact that God is able. But is he *willing*? Now, that's a good question. The answer is found in the relation between Jude 24 and Jude 25. Would God be deserving of such praise and honor if he were merely a God of power but not of purpose? If he were merely a God who *can* but *won't* keep his people from stumbling, would he be deserving of worship? What if he were merely a God of ability but lacked affection for his people? What possible good is it if God can preserve us but declines to do so? Is that kind of God worthy of the praise we read about in verse 25? Hardly. Can you imagine God saying, "Well, yes, of course I'm able to keep you from stumbling and to present you before me with joy, but I have no intention of doing so. In fact, I'm not in the least inclined to help you. As far as I'm concerned, you're on your own. Good luck. But don't look to me for help." Is that kind of God worthy of praise?

CONCLUSION

I can think of no better conclusion to our examination of these many texts that affirm the security of the saints' salvation than to cry out as Jude did: "Now to him who is able to keep you from stumbling and to present you blameless before the presence of his glory with great joy, to the only God, our Savior, through Jesus Christ our Lord, *be glory, majesty, dominion, and authority, before all time and now and forever. Amen."*

9

WARNINGS, PERPLEXING PASSAGES, AND THE POTENTIAL FOR APOSTASY, PART 1

If there were no such thing as so-called problem passages, the debate over the security of the saints would be over before it began. But the fact is, there are several biblical texts that on first reading appear to undermine the joy of assurance and the security of the believer's relationship to Christ. These passages speak of the potential for "falling away" and being "cut off" from the saving benefits of Christ's work. So how can one maintain a belief in the safety and security of the born-again believer in the face of such warnings? Therein lies the challenge that I will take up in these last three chapters.

ROMANS 11:22

We begin in Romans, which appears to provide the strongest evidence in support of the perseverance of the saints. Yet in Romans 11 Paul warns his readers that "if Jews who fell prey to unbelief were not spared God's judgment, then neither will Gentiles who succumb to unbelief escape his wrath."[1]

---

[1] Thomas R. Schreiner, *Romans*, Baker Exegetical Commentary on the New Testament (Grand Rapids, MI: Baker, 1998), 607.

> Note then the kindness and the severity of God: severity toward those who have fallen, but God's kindness to you, provided you continue in his kindness. Otherwise you too will be cut off. (Rom. 11:22)

Does that verse imply that genuine believers can lose their salvation? Three views are possible.

It may be that Paul is echoing a theme found elsewhere in his letters and throughout the New Testament, a theme that we've touched on repeatedly, namely, *that ultimate salvation is dependent on perseverance in faith* (cf. Rom. 8:13; Col. 1:23; Heb. 3:6, 14; 1 Pet. 1:5; 1 John 2:19), a faith that God graciously sustains within us.

Others have suggested that Paul's discussion here is about Gentiles as a class, considered collectively, and Israel as a class, considered collectively. In other words, just as Israel was cut off because of unbelief, so also Gentiles may be if they do not believe. According to this view, those who were cut off were not born-again believers but were Jews who, by virtue of their ethnicity, were members of the covenant community of Israel. Their unbelief was their rejection of Jesus as Messiah. Thus they were members of the one "olive tree" (v. 24) but did not experience saving faith. The breaking off of such branches was the corporate rejection of Israel. Could it be, then, that the threatened breaking off of Gentile branches should likewise be viewed as a corporate judgment? Doug Moo has another, far more probable, explanation:

> While the olive tree represents the true, spiritual people of God, those who are said to belong to this tree are not only those who, through their faith, are actually part of the tree but also those who only appear to belong to that tree. This is evident from the fact that Paul speaks of unbelieving Jews as having been "cut off" from the tree (v. 17). In reality, these Jews had never been part of the tree at all; yet to preserve the metaphor he is using, Paul presents them as if they had been. In the same

way, then, those Gentiles within the church at Rome—and elsewhere—who appear to be part of God's people, yet do not continue in faith, may never have been part of that tree at all.[2]

In a sermon on Romans 11, John Piper agrees: Paul "means that, on the one hand, *there are real, genuine, spiritual, inward attachments to the tree*—the covenant of grace and salvation; and, on the other hand, *there are unreal, counterfeit, unspiritual, outward attachments to the covenant.*" Failure or refusal to "continue in his [God's] kindness" (Rom. 11:22b) shows "that their attachment is merely external and unspiritual and non-transforming, and they will be cut off."[3]

The future tense "will be cut off" likely points to the day of final judgment, much the way Jesus referred to this in Matthew 7:22–23: "On that day many will say to me, 'Lord, Lord, did we not prophesy in your name, and cast out demons in your name, and do many mighty works in your name?' And then will I declare to them, 'I never knew you; depart from me, you workers of lawlessness.'" Piper says that in that declaration, "we hear the terrible squeezing of the omnipotent clippers lopping a fruitless, unspiritual, hypocritical church-going Christian from all attachment to the family of God."[4] So, "listen carefully and lay this to heart: Just as in the Old Testament you could be a circumcised, sacrifice-offering, outwardly law-abiding, physical child of Abraham and not a spiritual child of Abraham (John 8:39–44; Rom. 9:8), so in the New Testament church . . . you can be a baptized, communion-taking, worship-attending, tithe-giving, doctrine-affirming church member and not be a child of God."[5]

Thus, the first and third views may be combined. Those who have truly believed *will* continue in God's kindness (Heb. 3:6, 14). Those who do not continue in God's kindness show thereby that

[2] Douglas J. Moo, *The Epistle to the Romans*, New International Commentary on the New Testament (Grand Rapids, MI: Eerdmans, 1996), 707.
[3] John Piper, "You Stand Fast through Faith, So Do Not Become Proud, but Fear," sermon, February 8, 2004, http://www.desiringgod.org (emphasis original).
[4] Ibid.
[5] Ibid.

they were only superficially, but not savingly, part of the tree (see especially 1 John 2:19). Failure to persevere does not mean that one who was truly saved becomes truly lost. Rather, perseverance is itself the proof that one was truly saved. If one does not persevere, that one has always been lost and never saved. As Schreiner notes, "No one can presume upon God's grace and imagine that blessing will be theirs regardless of their continuance in faith."[6]

ROMANS 14:15

In Romans 14:15 Paul speaks about a strong Christian destroying a weaker Christian through the unloving exercise of freedom. He refers to a "stumbling block" in verse 13 and to hurting and destroying one's brother in verse 15. What does he mean? Certainly it is more than the emotional distress, pain, or annoyance that the weak brother feels on seeing a strong brother partake of food or drink that he believes is unclean and forbidden. Rather, Paul envisions a situation in which a strong Christian, in the exercise of his liberty, causes a weak Christian to sin. The weak brother sins when he is influenced, by the strong brother's behavior, to act contrary to his conscience. Paul envisions the grievous vexation of conscience that afflicts a believer when he violates what for him is the moral will of God. Paul's advice to the strong is simple: when the exercise of your legitimate liberty emboldens the weak to violate his conscience, you must defer to his interests and refrain from what would otherwise be permissible for you to do.

Paul's appeal to the death of Christ is penetrating. Here is how John Murray explains it:

> If Christ loved the weak believer to the extent of laying down his life for his salvation, how alien to the demands of this love is the refusal on the part of the strong to [forgo] the use of a certain article of food when the religious interests of the one

---

[6] Schreiner, *Romans*, 607.

for whom Christ died are thereby imperiled! It is the contrast between what the extreme sacrifice of Christ exemplified and the paltry demand devolving upon us that accentuates the meanness of our attitude when we discard the interests of a weak brother. And since the death of Christ as the price of redemption for all believers is the bond uniting them in fellowship, how contradictory is any behavior that is not patterned after the love which Christ's death exhibited![7]

If you are convinced that the request to suspend the exercise of your freedom for the sake of your brother is a great and unjust imposition, think of what Christ did.

Our primary concern, however, is whether the *destruction* here is eternal. There are several reasons why I believe that is not what Paul has in view.

First, John Stott rightly asks: "Are we really to believe that a Christian brother's single act against his own conscience—which in any case is not his fault but the fault of the strong who have misled him, and which is therefore an unintentional mistake, not a deliberate disobedience—merits eternal condemnation? No, hell is reserved only for the stubborn, the impenitent, those who willfully persist in wrongdoing."[8]

Second, Paul has just affirmed in unequivocal terms the eternal security of the believer (Rom. 8:28–39). If nothing in all creation can separate one from the love of Christ, then surely another believer's callous disregard for a weak brother's religious scruples cannot do so.

Third, Paul says in verse 15 that a Christian can "destroy" another Christian. This cannot refer to eternal destruction because Jesus said that God alone destroys body and soul in hell (see Matt. 10:28).

Fourth, Jesus said explicitly in John 10:28 that his sheep will "never perish." Clearly, then, the destruction in Romans 14:15 must

---

[7] John Murray, *The Epistle to the Romans*, vol. 2 (Grand Rapids, MI: Eerdmans, 1965), 191.
[8] John R. W. Stott, *Romans: God's Good News for the World* (Downers Grove, IL: InterVarsity, 1994), 365–66.

refer to something less than and different from the loss of eternal salvation.

Fifth, the context provides a perfectly reasonable explanation of Paul's words. He envisions serious damage to both the conscience of the weak believer (v. 15) and to his growth as a disciple of Jesus. Judith Gundry-Volf identifies two forms of damage incurred by the weak:

> A subjective form consisting in grief and deep self-depreca-tion, and an objective form consisting in concrete sin, resultant guilt and possible incapacitation to behave consistently with one's beliefs. None of Paul's descriptions of the negative conse-quences born by the weak when they follow the example of the strong—stumbling, sinning, sorrow, defiling and wounding of the conscience [cf. 1 Cor. 8:7], self-condemnation—necessarily entails loss of salvation or complete dissolution of a relation-ship to God.[9]

It appears best to conclude, therefore, that the "destruction" pres-ents an obstacle to one's *sanctification*, not to one's *justification*.

1 CORINTHIANS 9:24–27

Do you not know that in a race all the runners run, but only one receives the prize? So run that you may obtain it. Every athlete exercises self-control in all things. They do it to receive a perishable wreath, but we an imperishable. So I do not run aimlessly; I do not box as one beating the air. But I discipline my body and keep it under control, lest after preaching to oth-ers I myself should be disqualified. (1 Cor. 9:24–27)

If the "prize" to which Paul refers in verse 24 is the consummation of our salvation in the eternal state, and if being "disqualified" in verse

---

[9] Judith Gundry-Volf, *Paul and Perseverance: Staying In and Falling Away* (Louisville, KY: Westminster, 1990), 95.

27 has in view eternal condemnation, must we conclude that Paul envisions the possibility of a born-again believer suffering the loss of his salvation? I don't think so.

Once again, as we saw in Romans 11:22, it may be that Paul is echoing a theme found elsewhere in his letters and throughout the New Testament, namely, *that ultimate salvation is dependent on perseverance in faith* (cf. Rom. 8:13; Col. 1:23; Heb. 3:6, 14; 1 Pet. 1:5; 1 John 2:19), which Paul believes God graciously preserves and sustains within us.

We must never lose sight of what Paul said earlier in 1 Corinthians. In 1:8 the apostle assures believers in Corinth that God "will sustain you to the end, guiltless in the day of our Lord Jesus Christ." This promise is one on which we can rest assured, because the God who called us is "faithful" (v. 9). That is to say, he will always prove faithful to supply us with the spiritual energy to continue to believe, a belief on which our ultimate salvation is suspended. Final salvation depends on enduring faith, a faith that God himself has pledged that he will uphold and preserve in our hearts. As we've seen, that doesn't mean a believer cannot trip and tumble, digress and doubt, perhaps even backslide for a season. But it does mean that no true child of God can fall so as to fully and finally fail to finish the race.

Thus, what Paul says in 1 Corinthians 9 must be consistent with what he said in chapter 1. Knowing this to be true, observes John Piper, Paul is simply reaffirming that "the race of life has eternal consequences *not because grace is nullified by the way we run, but because grace is verified by the way we run. . . .* Paul's running did not nullify the purpose of grace; it verified the power of grace."[10] That is to say, "eternal life hangs on the way we run and the way we fight not because salvation is based on the merit of works, but because faith without works is dead (James 2:26). Life is a proving ground

[10] John Piper, "Olympic Spirituality, Part 1," August 2, 1992, and "Olympic Spirituality, Part 2," August 9, 1992, sermons, http://www.desiringgod.org (emphasis added).

for whether faith is alive or dead—a proving ground for whom we trust."[11]

Failing to finish the race because of injury or perhaps veering off course and crossing over into another runner's lane will, in the world of track and field, lead to almost certain disqualification. Paul appears to be drawing on this analogy to make his case that if we hope to receive the prize of full and final salvation, we too must endure to the end; we too must not run so as to suffer expulsion.

This doesn't mean that he envisions the possibility of a genuine born-again child of God failing to do so and thus suffering eternal damnation. Divine provision has been made in the form of Paul's urgent plea that we exercise spiritual self-control and discipline ourselves to maintain our course in life. Such are the instrumental means of personal endurance in faith. They are the way in which we are assured of final salvation. And the glorious news that we have repeatedly seen throughout the New Testament is that God has pledged to be antecedent to this requirement, working in advance to supply us with his Spirit and sustain us in faith and energize us to endure in confident hope in all that he has done for us in Christ. Running as fast as grace empowers us and enduring by God's Spirit to the end of the race are together the proof that Christ is in us and that we are, by genuine saving faith, in him. As Piper explains:

> Life is not a game with no lasting consequences. The way we live our lives has eternal consequences. Life is a proving ground where we prove who we are, whom we trust, and what we cherish. Eternal life, the upward call, the crown of righteousness— all these hang on what our life says about who we are, whom we trust, and what we love. Make no mistake here! Life is not a place for proving to God or anybody your strength. Life is a place for proving whose strength you trust—man's or God's. Life is not a place for proving the power of your intelligence to

---

[11] Ibid.

know truth. It's a place for proving the power of God's grace to show truth (Matt. 16:17). Life is not a field for demonstrating the force of our will to make good choices. It's a field for showing how the beauty of Christ takes us captive and constrains us to choose and run for his glory. The race of life has eternal consequences, not because we are saved by works, but because Christ has saved us from dead works to serve the living and true God with Olympic passion (Heb. 9:14).[12]

Another view, however, is that Paul's concern is that he not become slack or indifferent in his ministry lest he forfeit God's approval on his apostolic endeavors (and perhaps the power of the Holy Spirit that energizes his work). He fears not hearing God say, "Well done, good and faithful servant" and thereby forfeiting the divine blessings and rewards he otherwise would receive (a theme he earlier addressed in 1 Cor. 3:10–15). On this reading, the Greek word *adokimos* (translated "disqualified") does not pertain to the test of faith but to the test of apostleship. In 2 Corinthians Paul applies the terminology of testing (*adokimos* and its cognates) to himself *as an apostle*, not as a professing Christian (see 13:6–7; cf. 1 Thess. 2:4; 2 Tim. 2:15). Gundry-Volf, an advocate of this interpretation, concludes:

> The fact that no instance of the use of *adokimos* or a cognate referring to Paul relates to the test of faith or salvation, rather, that every instance has to do with his fitness as an apostle raises doubts about the view that *adokimos* in 1 Cor. 9:27 means rejected from salvation and suggests instead that it means rejected as an apostle.[13]

In either case, there is no reason to conclude from 1 Corinthians 9 that a justified child of God can ever fully and finally fall from the saving arms of Christ.

---

[12] Ibid.
[13] Gundry-Volf, *Paul and Perseverance*, 236–37.

2 CORINTHIANS 6:1–2

What does Paul mean when he refers to the possibility of receiving the grace of God "in vain" (v. 1)?[14] There have been several suggested proposals.

Perhaps Paul is urging the Corinthians not to forfeit the grace of salvation, which they had earlier received. In other words, it is an exhortation to persevere and thus to avoid apostasy. According to this view, the apostle is implying that a born-again believer can lose or forfeit his or her salvation.

Some suggest that the exhortation in verses 1–2 is not directed to the Corinthians who are already born again but to those in Corinth who had repeatedly heard the gospel but had made no decision. Paul was not so naïve as to think that everyone in the *professing* church was truly converted. Therefore, his command not to receive the grace of God in vain is equivalent to an exhortation to all men not to reject the gospel of Jesus Christ. But is "to receive in vain" really the same as "reject"?

God's grace may be received in vain if it is received superficially or externally, as in the parable of the soils (Luke 8:4–15; Matt. 13:18–23). There the seed (gospel) falls upon rocky ground or among thorns, to be snatched away or choked by the temptations of the world. This view is similar to the previous one, insofar as the people in view are unbelievers. The difference is that here people don't explicitly reject the gospel but "receive" and "believe" it yet only in a superficial way. Their so-called faith is spurious and therefore temporary (a theme we saw in several instances from John's Gospel).

Perhaps receiving the grace of God in vain pertains not so much to salvation or its forfeiture but to the loss of potential blessings related to spiritual growth, knowledge, and joy they would suffer by rejecting Paul as their apostle. In other words, the people are truly saved. They have genuinely received the gospel and believed it, but

---

[14] See also Gal. 2:2; Phil. 2:16; 1 Thess. 3:5 (cf. 1 Cor. 15:2).

they have failed to progress in their Christian growth and stand in danger of losing those spiritual blessings and rewards they otherwise might have obtained.

Philip Hughes suggests that "for them to receive the grace of God in vain meant that their practice did not measure up to their profession as Christians, that their lives were so inconsistent as to constitute a denial of the logical implications of the gospel, namely, and in particular, that Christ died for them so that they might no longer live to themselves but to His glory."[15] In other words, the passionate conviction that accompanied their salvation had not as yet performed its transforming work in their lives. It is to that progressive transformation of their daily experience that Paul is exhorting them. In the final analysis, this view differs very little from the fourth one cited above.

Judith Gundry-Volf suggests that Paul's admonition not to receive the grace of God in vain may involve their opposition to the apostle himself. The context of this statement is Paul's description of his ministry on their behalf and his attempt to restore good relations with them (5:13–14; 5:18–6:1; see especially his impassioned appeal in 6:11–13). In Paul's opinion, to reject *him* is to reject the gospel of salvation of which he is a minister. If the Corinthians receive the grace of God in vain, it is not because of ethical failure or moral rebellion but as a consequence of rejection of the apostle and the apostolic message. Gundry-Volf then argues that Paul's appeal is simply *"for the sake of argument only."*[16] In other words, he does not believe they will reject or deny him, but if they were to do so, it would be tantamount to receiving the grace of God, which was his message to them, in vain.

---

[15] Philip Edgcumbe Hughes, *Paul's Second Epistle to the Corinthians* (Grand Rapids, MI: Eerdmans, 1973), 218–19.

[16] Gundry-Volf, *Paul and Perseverance*, 280 (emphasis original).

GALATIANS 5:2–4

> Look: I, Paul, say to you that if you accept circumcision, Christ will be of no advantage to you. I testify again to every man who accepts circumcision that he is obligated to keep the whole law. You are severed from Christ, you who would be justified by the law; you have fallen away from grace. (Gal. 5:2–4)

Here the apostle refers to some in the church at Galatia who were considering circumcision, having believed the Judaizers' heretical doctrine that such works were necessary to bring their salvation in Christ to its proper consummation. If a person were to embrace this doctrine and implement it, says Paul, "Christ will be of no advantage" (v. 2). Furthermore, to submit to circumcision is to submit to the obligation "to keep the whole law" (v. 3). Those who seek to be justified by law have been "severed from Christ" and "have fallen away from grace" (v. 4).

Before we go any further, it's important that we not make the mistake of imposing our way of speaking in the twenty-first-century church onto the biblical text. In other words, we cannot simply assume that our contemporary understanding of "falling from grace" is identical to what Paul intended when he wrote his letter to the Galatians. Virtually all Christians from every conceivable tradition typically associate the words "falling from grace" as a reference to the loss of salvation. That may also be what Paul had in mind, but it is not the interpretation of all biblical scholars. We must not think that our theological categories and the meaning with which we fill them is always identical to those of the New Testament authors. That being said, we are prepared to look at this notoriously difficult passage.

The Arminian interpretation is that Paul envisions true Christians apostatizing from the faith and being cut off from the saving grace of God, which they once genuinely experienced. They once were saved. Now they are lost.

The Calvinist recognizes three alternate possibilities.

First, some insist that these whom Paul describes are not, in point of fact, real Christians. They are professing believers who have identified externally with the church in Galatia (not an uncommon phenomenon in the first—or any—century). Their lack of true, saving faith in Jesus is demonstrated by their desire to be justified in God's sight through works, circumcision in particular. Christ cannot be of saving benefit to someone who refuses to submit to him and to the way of salvation he has ordained: by grace alone through faith alone. To seek justification by obedience to the law ("you who would be justified by the law," v. 4) is to be cut off from the saving work of Christ. It is to fall from that principle of divine grace by which one may alone be saved. It is an issue of which means of acceptance with God you choose: grace or law.

Such people fall from grace and into legalism, not from salvation into condemnation. Advocates of this view quickly point out the contrast Paul draws between people who pursue acceptance with God by such legal means and "we" (true believers) in verse 5, who "by faith" are waiting for the consummation of our salvation.

Second, others concede that those Paul describes are genuine Christians, but what they forfeit isn't salvation but the experiential blessings of intimacy with God that are grounded on and flow from the reliance of the soul on grace alone. Thus, being severed from Christ and falling from grace refer to the loss of joy, fellowship, reward, and blessing but not the loss of one's place in the kingdom of God.

Third, a more likely interpretation is that Paul is addressing genuine but immature believers who, in the words of Bruce Demarest, were about "to defect from a *theology* of justification by grace to a theology of justification by law-keeping. They were running the race well until the Judaizers caused them to turn aside."[17] Paul has con-

---

[17] Bruce Demarest, *The Cross and Salvation: The Doctrine of Salvation*, Foundations of Evangelical Theology (Wheaton, IL: Crossway, 1997), 456 (emphasis original).

fidence "in the Lord" (v. 10); in other words, because of who Christ
is and because of his commitment to his people, the erring saints
would soon return to the truth of the principle of justification by
grace alone through faith alone in Christ alone.

Gundry-Volf, on the other hand, believes it is from more than a
principle of grace that they stand to fall—it is from grace itself. In
other words, they abandon and are severed from the very foundation of their salvation. But she agrees with Demarest that such will
not, in point of fact, ever happen. Paul's declaration of confidence is
crucial to this understanding. Notwithstanding the severe warning
(vv. 2–4), Paul writes:

> I have confidence in the Lord that you will take no other view
> [than mine], and the one who is troubling you [a collective al-
> lusion to the Judaizers] will bear the penalty, whoever he is.
> (v. 10)

Says Gundry-Volf:

> Paul not only *hopes* that his warnings and pleadings will evoke
> the desired response. He claims to "have been persuaded in the
> Lord concerning you that you will think nothing other" than
> the truth (5:10). Though he anathematizes the perpetrators of
> the "other gospel" (1:8, 9) and consigns them to "judgment"
> (5:10), regarding them as "false brethren" (cf. 2:4), he has confi-
> dence that his Galatian converts will reaffirm their acceptance
> of the gospel he preached to them.[18]

Thus, the key to Paul's confidence is found in the words "in the
Lord." In other words,

> After all Paul's efforts to mend the situation, he acknowledges
> that the Galatians' destiny does not lie in his hands but the
> Lord's. And the Lord's faithfulness guarantees the final out-

---

[18] Gundry-Volf, *Paul and Perseverance*, 214 (emphasis original).

come. . . . Paul's own intervention in the matter is not thereby rendered superfluous, however. For God's faithfulness can manifest itself precisely in the effect the apostle's warning and wooing has in the Galatian churches. . . . From the perspective of God's faithfulness, Paul is certain that the Galatians will not finally turn away from the gospel.[19]

Thus Paul envisions the faithfulness of God to his people as being greater and more powerful than the threat to their salvation. Paul's confidence is in the God who works and sustains in spite of human failure. As F. F. Bruce puts it, Paul "knows how the logic of the gospel works, and if they have really received the gospel (as he is convinced they have), they must accept the same logic and think no differently . . . from himself."[20]

In sum, the threat is real. True Christians are often tempted to turn away from the grace by which they are saved. To do so would be eternally disastrous. But God is faithful to preserve us. Therefore, in the words of the apostle Peter, we "are being guarded through faith for a salvation ready to be revealed in the last time" (1 Pet. 1:5). It is ultimately God's power, not ours, that ever energizes and upholds our faith in Christ.

The standard objection to this way of thinking points out that, contrary to what one might contend, the threat, in point of fact, is *not* real. If God has guaranteed the saints' perseverance in faith, no threat can pose any danger to their eternal security. Such a guarantee thus empties any so-called warning of its practical value.

The most articulate response to this objection comes from Thomas Schreiner.[21] He understands that the Galatians' desire to be circumcised reflects a desire to be under the law as a whole (see Gal.

---

[19] Ibid., 215.

[20] F. F. Bruce, *The Epistle to the Galatians: A Commentary on the Greek Text* (Grand Rapids, MI: Eerdmans, 1982), 235.

[21] In addition to his commentary on Galatians, Tom's view has been clearly defended in two books that I noted earlier: Thomas R. Schreiner and Ardel B. Caneday, *The Race Set Before Us: A Biblical Theology of Perseverance and Assurance* (Downers Grove: InterVarsity, 2001); Thomas R. Schreiner, *Run to Win the Prize: Perseverance in the New Testament* (Wheaton, IL: Crossway, 2010).

4:21). But "circumcision only 'profits' . . . if one keeps the entire law (Rom. 2:25). Those who are circumcised and fail to observe the law become like uncircumcised Gentiles, i.e., outside of God's covenant people."[22] The reason this is such a weighty matter is that "if they rely on circumcision for salvation, they cannot lean on Christ for the same. No middle way exists between circumcision and Christ. If the Galatians turn to circumcision, they lose Christ and all his benefits."[23]

Schreiner contends that "Paul does not declare here that the Galatians *have* definitively fallen from grace. . . . It seems more likely . . . that Paul asserts what will be the case *if* the Galatians revert to the law."[24] Thus they have not, in actual fact, been justified by the law but are attempting to do so (hence the rendering "you who *would be* justified by the law"). By warning them of the consequences of such apostasy, namely, that all such folk will thereby fall from grace and forfeit their salvation, the Galatians are awakened from their spiritual deception and are provoked to persevere in their trust in Christ alone. Such warnings are "the means God uses to preserve the faith of those whom he has chosen."[25] If the Galatians or any who profess Christ revert to reliance on the law for acceptance with God, they therein renounce Christ and lose all hope for salvation on the final day. The warning is thus designed to incite his readers "to keep trusting Christ until the end, so that they do not turn to other gods for deliverance."[26]

But is it not the case that all who trust Christ *cannot*, in fact, turn to other gods (such as circumcision and the law) for deliverance, and that those who do therein demonstrate that they never did trust Christ in the first place? Schreiner would agree but argues that "the warnings are one of the means God uses to keep us in the good way

---

[22] Thomas R. Schreiner, *Galatians: Zondervan Exegetical Commentary on the New Testament* (Grand Rapids, MI: Zondervan, 2010), 313.
[23] Ibid.
[24] Ibid., 315 (emphasis original).
[25] Ibid., 318.
[26] Ibid., 319.

of trusting in Christ. Warnings are not opposed to promises, but are one of the means God uses to fulfill his promises."[27] Yes, but is this not a warning to beware of something happening that God has promised never will?

Schreiner seeks to escape this problem with an illustration that he believes is parallel to the spiritual issue we are discussing. He describes how friends who were visiting his home parked their van in the back of the Schreiner driveway. Tom joked one day that he might crash into the van as he was pulling out of the garage. Sure enough, a day later his family piled into the car, and he backed out quickly. Suddenly, Tom's son yelled out, "Dad. Stop!" Tom slammed on the brakes and barely avoided the impending crash. Tom contends that his son's warning "was the means by which I avoided an accident. That's how God's warnings work too. They prevent us from falling away from Christ."[28]

I'm not entirely confident that this illustration is sufficiently analogous to explain the validity of such warnings in Scripture. We must remember that there was nothing to guarantee that Tom could never hit the van. It was always *possible* that he might crash into it. But in the case of the born-again believer's relationship to God, our Father has guaranteed that it is impossible to be cut off from Christ. Any warning that such will happen if we apostatize is meaningless if the one issuing the warning has previously and on numerous occasions assured us that he will faithfully work in our hearts to ensure that apostasy can never occur.

As you can see from these multiple and diverse interpretations, this is a notoriously difficult text to understand. Nevertheless, given the overwhelming clarity of Paul's teaching in his other epistles, not to mention what we find in John 6 and 10, I cannot embrace the Arminian argument that the apostle here envisions the true believer falling from saving grace into eternal damnation. Although I'm not

---

[27] Ibid.
[28] Ibid., 320.

entirely satisfied with any of the interpretive options suggested by Calvinist scholars, one of them must surely be correct.

COLOSSIANS 1:23 [29]

In his epistle to the Colossians Paul writes that believers persevere, "if indeed you continue in the faith, stable and steadfast, not shifting from the hope of the gospel that you heard, which has been proclaimed in all creation under heaven, and of which I, Paul, became a minister" (1:23). Paul seems clearly to say that if you don't persevere by continuing in the faith, you will not be presented before God holy and blameless and without reproach. Whether "the faith" is a reference to one's personal trust in Jesus or the objective body of truths we call "the Christian faith," the fact remains: if you don't continue in it, you will not experience the inestimable joy of standing forever in the presence of God.

So, yes, there is truly a conditional element involved ("if indeed"). The condition for final presentation is faithful perseverance. The notion espoused by some that one "act of faith" in Jesus Christ eternally secures final salvation, irrespective of how one lives, is unbiblical. But that's for another day.

Having said this, three options are worthy of our consideration. There are probably others, but I want to focus on three.

First, the Arminian view says it is possible for the truly regenerate (born again) soul to fail to meet the condition and thereby fail to be presented holy and blameless and without reproach before God. The salvation once gained by faith alone may be forfeited by the death of said faith.

Second, some Calvinists read Colossians 1:23 as saying that perseverance is the proof that one's "act of faith" in Jesus Christ was genuine. Perseverance, or continuing stable and steadfast in the faith, not shifting from the hope of the gospel, is evidence of the

---

[29] Much of this discussion has been adapted from my book *The Hope of Glory: 100 Daily Meditations on Colossians* (Wheaton, IL: Crossway, 2008), 116–19. Used by permission of Crossway.

authenticity of one's initial conversion and commitment to Christ. Likewise, the failure to persevere is proof that one's profession of faith in Jesus was false, an act of self-delusion.

This concept is undoubtedly true, in my opinion, and other biblical texts that we've examined clearly affirm it. The passage in 1 John 2:19 speaks to this scenario. There John writes, "They [i.e., the false teachers] went out from us, but they were not of us; for if they had been of us, they would have continued with us. But they went out, that it might become plain that they all are not of us." So again, endurance is the sign of the saved, just as apostasy reveals the counterfeit character of one's initial profession of faith. The presence of saving faith ("of us") implies (indeed, necessitates) perseverance.

Third, the other Calvinist option (similar to the one offered by Schreiner) interprets Paul's purpose in Colossians 1:23 somewhat differently. All Calvinists believe that the elect will fully and finally persevere and thus be eternally saved (in fact, some Arminians believe this too). They will not fail to fulfill the condition of Colossians 1:23. But, according to this third option, God preserves us in faith and holiness of life by stirring our hearts to avail ourselves of his sustaining grace. One way he does this is *by means of the warning implicit in the condition.* The warning is simply this: no continuation, no presentation. In other words, God keeps us safe, and thus we persevere by heeding the warning that if we don't, we will not be presented blameless and without reproach before God.

Both Calvinist options hold that the elect will persevere. According to the first, Colossians 1:23 looks backward. As we consider whether a person continues in the faith, we are directed to draw one of two conclusions concerning the authenticity of their initial profession of trust in Jesus.

According to the second view, Colossians 1:23 looks forward. Christian, take heed to this undeniable fact: if you don't persevere by continuing in the faith, you won't be presented before God. Christian, take heart in knowing that God will work in you "that which is pleasing in his sight" (see Heb. 13:21). Be encouraged with the assurance that he who began a good work in you will bring it to completion at the day of Jesus Christ (Phil. 1:6), so that you will persevere and not shift from the hope of the gospel which you believed.

As noted in our discussion of Galatians 5, some insist that the assurance that God will preserve us undermines the urgency to make certain that we continue in our faith. Many Calvinists argue precisely the opposite. The reason we commit ourselves fervently to the pursuit of holiness of life is that God has assured us that he will be ever present to energize our hearts "to will and to work for his good pleasure" (Phil. 2:12–13). Praise God for his preserving presence and power!

If you are inclined to indulge in unrepentant sin and then justify your licentiousness on the grounds that God has promised to preserve you, there is a strong likelihood that your alleged faith in Christ is not saving faith. Given what Paul says in Colossians 1:23, I would be irresponsible to assure you that by pursuing such a life you will, nevertheless, be presented before him holy and blameless and without reproach. Remember: no continuation, no presentation.

1 TIMOTHY 1:18–20

A number of people have concluded from 1 Timothy 1:18–20 that a true believer can apostatize and lose his or her salvation. Is that what it really says? Paul writes:

> This charge I entrust to you, Timothy, my child, in accordance with the prophecies previously made about you, that by them you may wage the good warfare, holding faith and a good conscience. By rejecting this, some have made shipwreck of their faith, among whom are Hymenaeus and Alexander, whom I have handed over to Satan that they may learn not to blaspheme. (1 Tim. 1:18–20)

We must first ask, Were Hymenaeus and Alexander saved? It's

difficult to say. There is no way of knowing whether their presence in the church at Ephesus was an external association based on their verbal profession of faith or an internal, spiritual union with the body of Christ. We are told that they rejected a good conscience and as a result suffered shipwreck in regard to their faith. As Stott has said, "If we disregard the voice of conscience, allowing sin to remain unconfessed and unforsaken, our faith will not long survive."[30]

Paul took disciplinary action by delivering them over to Satan so that "they may learn not to blaspheme" (v. 20). Certainly believers are capable of backsliding and doing serious damage to their fellowship with Christ, and believers are capable of falling into serious doctrinal error, becoming subject to excommunication. The imagery of a shipwreck suggests serious damage but need not imply the loss of salvation. The purpose in Paul's action, to teach them not to blaspheme, is consistent with how a believer adhering to doctrinal error should be viewed. Thus Paul's disciplinary action had as its purpose the restoration of a wayward brother (see a similar situation in 1 Corinthians 5).

On the other hand, they may well have been nonbelievers. In rejecting a good conscience they made shipwreck of, literally, *the* faith, i.e., the truths of Christianity objectively considered. If this were the case, Paul's words may be a description of their willful repudiation of the truth of the gospel, resulting in their expulsion from the church. The bottom line, however, is that nothing in the passage states these men were born-again believers who lost their salvation.

2 TIMOTHY 2:11–13

Concerning Jesus, Paul declares, "If we deny him, he also will deny us" (2 Tim. 2:12). Paul is simply echoing Jesus's statement in Matthew 10:32–33: "So everyone who acknowledges me before men, I also will acknowledge before My Father who is in heaven, but who-

---

[30] John R. W. Stott, *Guard the Truth: The Message of 1 Timothy and Titus* (Downers Grove, IL: InterVarsity, 1996), 57.

ever denies me before men, I also will deny before my Father who is in heaven." Make no mistake about it: to deny Jesus, to declare that he is not the Son of God incarnate, that he did not die for sinners and rise from the dead, and that he is not the only way to the Father, results in eternal death. Anyone who denies the Son shall himself be denied.

Paul's use of the first-person plural "we" is simply a standard conversational convention or literary form found throughout the New Testament and used by everyone, even today. It is what might be called the "preacher's we" in which the speaker or writer addresses his audience collectively. Jesus used the words "everyone" and "whoever" because he was himself the object of either the affirmation or the denial under consideration. Paul does not have that luxury and thus makes use of a literary custom to drive home his point. *Whoever* denies the Son, regardless of their prior profession of faith, is lost. Someone who professes faith in Jesus and later blatantly and persistently denies him only proves that his earlier profession was that—merely words. For other examples of the "preacher's we" in a warning passage, see Hebrews 2:3 and 12:25.

The "preacher's we" is used frequently today as well. When I speak to an audience in which I suspect are both Christians and non-Christians (most likely *all* audiences contain both), I say something like this: "People, hear me well. If we believe in Jesus, we will be saved. However, if we turn our back on him and the offer of life that is based on his atoning sacrifice, we will be forever lost." In using such terms ("if" and "we") I'm not suggesting that I don't already believe in Jesus or that I might deny him in the future. It is an appeal and a warning to anyone and everyone in which fundamental truths and their consequences are stated.

Be it also noted that Paul does not have in mind the kind of denial into which Peter fell. In Peter's case, the denial was momentary and was followed by great remorse and repentance. The denial Paul has in view in 2 Timothy is both persistent and final, an utter and absolute repudiation of Jesus. Says George Knight:

> The statement in the saying that we are now considering does not mean that Christ is not faithful to his promise to us, nor does it mean that our fall into a denial even as grave as Peter's is unforgivable or that it from that time henceforth forever and ever seals our doom. The denial in view in the saying which calls forth Christ's denial is not like that of Peter's who later sought forgiveness but rather is a situation of hardness and permanence.[31]

To be continued . . .

---

[31] George W. Knight, *The Faithful Sayings in the Pastoral Epistles* (Grand Rapids, MI: Baker, 1979), 126.

10

Warnings, Perplexing Passages, and the Potential for Apostasy, Part 2

In keeping with our subject matter, there are additional problem passages that must be addressed in what are known as the "General Epistles," together with one particular text in the book of Revelation. But first we must return to the book of Hebrews to take up a warning that has plagued interpreters for centuries.

Hebrews 10:26–31

In Hebrews 10:26–31 our author describes someone as continuing in willful sin "after receiving the knowledge of the truth," which might mean no more than that someone has heard and understood the gospel and given mental assent to it. Tragically, many people hear the good news and commit to shape their lives by the ethics of Jesus and in accordance with the standards and life of a local church while never experiencing regeneration and placing their personal trust in Christ for salvation. They then turn from what they have heard and understood and openly and defiantly repudiate it as false. There are unsaved theologians and biblical commentators whose knowledge of the truth of Christianity, at least in terms of objective data, is more extensive and insightful than that held by some true believers. The troubling phrase in this Hebrews passage occurs in verse 29, where one is said to have regarded as unclean "the blood of the covenant by which he was sanctified." Does this mean a genuine Christian is in view? Those who affirm eternal security have pointed to one of two possible interpretations.

First, some have suggested that the "he" who is sanctified is actually Jesus Christ, not the apostate, and such an interpretation is grammatically possible. It is also theologically possible, as John 17:19 speaks of Jesus "sanctifying" himself. We must remember that "to sanctify" can mean "to set apart for a special purpose or use" without the notion of sin being involved. We find similar language and thought in Hebrews 2:10; 5:7, 9; and 9:11–12. Noel Weeks argues:

> The whole point of the author has been to emphasize that Jesus has fulfilled the requirements of a High Priest. There is an analogy between the Aaronic ordinances and the sacrifice of Christ. So it is reasonable to suggest that as Aaron was consecrated by the blood of the sacrifice (Ex. 29), so Jesus was consecrated as High Priest through the offering of His own blood.[1]

Wayne Grudem and others contend that "the word *sanctified* need not refer to the internal moral purification that comes with salvation, for the term *hagiazo* has a broader range than that, both in Hebrews and in the New Testament generally."[2] Grudem points to Hebrews 9:13 as an example where the word refers to rendering someone ceremonially clean but not necessarily spiritually (or savingly) clean (see also Matt. 23:17, 19; 1 Cor. 7:14; and 1 Tim. 4:5). The context in Hebrews 10 appears to support this view, as our author is concerned with parallels between the Old Testament Levitical sacrifice and the better new-covenant sacrifice of Christ. Says Grudem:

---

[1] Noel Weeks, "Admonition and Error in Hebrews," *Westminster Theological Journal* 39 (Fall 1976): 80.
[2] Wayne Grudem, "Perseverance of the Saints: A Case Study from the Warning Passages in Hebrews," in *Still Sovereign: Contemporary Perspectives on Election, Foreknowledge, and Grace*, ed. Thomas R. Schreiner and Bruce A. Ware (Grand Rapids, MI: Baker, 2000), 177.

The author of Hebrews knows that some may fall away, even though *they assemble with the congregation of believers* and so share in this great privilege of coming before God [see 10:19–22]. So he says, "not neglecting to meet together, as is the habit of some, but encouraging one another" (10:25). The reason to encourage one another is the warning in 10:26, "For if we sin deliberately after receiving the knowledge of the truth." In such a context, it is appropriate to understand "profaned the blood of the covenant by which he was *sanctified*" to mean *"by which he was given the privilege of coming before God with the congregation of God's people."* In this sense, the blood of Christ opened up a new way of access to God for the congregation—it "sanctified" them in a parallel to the Old Testament ceremonial sense—and this person, by associating with the congregation, was also "sanctified" in that sense: He or she had the privilege of coming before God in worship.[3]

Someone who has experienced that awesome privilege only to willfully repudiate the person and work of Christ, through whom it was made possible, can expect only judgment. Consistent with this, our author then distinguishes between two groups in Hebrews 10:39. There are those who do not have saving faith and thus eventually fall away ("shrink back") into destruction and those who have saving faith and thus persevere to the preserving of the soul. He doesn't envision a third group: those who have saving faith and later fall away.

James 5:19–20

My brothers, if anyone among you wanders from the truth and someone brings him back, let him know that whoever brings back a sinner from his wandering will save his soul from death and will cover a multitude of sins. (James 5:19–20)

---

[3] Ibid., 178 (emphasis original).

In James 5:19–20 James encourages believers to call wayward believers back to the truth, which will "save his soul from death" and "cover a multitude of sins." However, this does not mean there is the potential for Christians to sin so severely that if someone *doesn't* intervene to restore them, they might lose their salvation. First, to wander "from the truth" (v. 19) refers to any form of departure from biblical standards, whether in thought (belief) or conduct. James probably has in mind someone rebellious and disobedient to the truths that he has set forth in this epistle.

Second, to bring him back means to restore him to the path of obedience and truth. James envisions one believer helping another believer to get back on the track of repentance and obedience.

Third, we need to determine whose soul is saved and whose sins are covered. Many say that both are those of the sinner who needs to be restored. Others contend that both clauses refer not to the sinner in need of restoration but to the Christian who is the means of the restoration. In other words, the salvation of his soul and the covering of his sins are in some sense a *reward* to the Christian for his work of restoring a wayward brother or sister. Others separate the two clauses: the one whose soul is saved is the restored sinner, but the one whose sins are covered is the Christian who has been the means of his recovery.

It is unlikely James is telling us that if we help restore a wayward brother, then *our* soul will be saved from death. After all, *we* are not straying from the truth and hence are not in danger of death. Most, then, agree that the one whose soul is saved is the brother who formerly strayed. Also, since it is a "sinner" (v. 20) who strayed and is now restored, it seems only reasonable that the sins covered are his. It doesn't make much sense that James would encourage the good work of restoring an errant brother in order to obtain forgiveness of our own sins. Therefore, the first view is the most likely: both the soul saved and the sins covered are those of the wayward brother or sister.

Fourth, the terms "save" and the "death" from which he is delivered (v. 20) must be identified. Just a few verses earlier, in 5:15, James used the term "save" to describe physical restoration from illness. The death in verse 20, therefore, is most likely physical, not spiritual, death (see also v. 12). Thus, James is encouraging us to be diligent to restore to repentance any brother or sister who has strayed from the truth. In doing so, we will have been instrumental in saving them from premature physical death (under the discipline of the Lord; cf. Acts 5; 1 Cor. 11:30–32). There is nothing in this passage that might lead us to believe a true Christian could lose his or her salvation.

2 Peter 2:20–22

Second Peter 2 is a graphic portrayal of the moral corruption and destructive influence of false teachers in the church. The problem for the doctrine of eternal security is the description in verses 20–22 of what appears to be irremediable apostasy. Peter speaks of people who

> if, after they have escaped the defilements of the world through the knowledge of our Lord and Savior Jesus Christ, they are again entangled in them and overcome, the last state has become worse for them than the first. For it would have been better for them never to have known the way of righteousness than after knowing it to turn back from the holy commandment delivered to them. What the true proverb says has happened to them: "The dog returns to its own vomit, and the sow, after washing herself, returns to wallow in the mire."

The terms used here appear to describe genuine conversion. Second Peter 1:4 refers to the salvation experience as one in which people have "escaped from the corruption that is in the world because of sinful desire." Likewise, they are said to have escaped the defilements of the world through the "knowledge" (2:20) of Jesus

Christ, a term Peter also uses in 2 Peter 1:2, 3, and 8 of those truly saved. Yet now we are told that they become entangled and overcome yet again by the defilements of the world and have turned back from the holy commandment delivered to them. Thus, their "last state has become worse for them than the first" (v. 20b). The first state refers to bondage to the defilements of the world. The last state points to their recent rejection of the faith. Concerning why the last state is worse than the first, Schreiner says it would appear to be "because those who had experienced the Christian faith and then rejected it were unlikely to return to it again. They would not grant a fresh hearing to the gospel, concluding that they had already been through 'that phase.'"[4]

Schreiner's explanation is that "the language in 2 Peter is *phenomenological*. In other words, Peter used the language of 'Christians' to describe those who fell away because they gave every appearance of being Christians. They confessed Christ as Lord and Savior, were baptized, and joined the church."[5] Thus Peter portrays them as if they were Christians "precisely because of their participation in the church, because they gave some evidence initially of genuine faith."[6] Douglas Moo, citing D. A. Carson, suggests:

> The New Testament consistently recognizes a class of people who are not simply pagans (that is, they are part of the church and have come to experience the blessings of Christ), but who are not yet regenerate Christians either (that is, the Hoy Spirit has not yet brought them to faith). Such people are difficult to recognize, and they may, indeed, only be known by their perseverance to the end. In other words, New Testament writers sometimes use the language of Christian conversion for such people on the basis of their appearance.[7]

---

[4] Thomas R. Schreiner, *1, 2 Peter, Jude*, New American Commentary (Nashville: Broadman, 2003), 361.
[5] Ibid., 364 (emphasis added).
[6] Ibid., 365.
[7] Douglas J. Moo, *2 Peter and Jude*, NIV Application Commentary (Grand Rapids, MI: Zondervan, 1996), 154.

That these false teachers are not now and never were truly converted is confirmed by the proverb Peter cites (Prov. 26:11). It's important to remember that among the Jews both dogs and pigs were
unclean animals. The former were not cute, loveable household pets
but typically roamed in packs, scavenging from garbage and filth.
The status of pigs in Jewish culture was anathema and hardly needs
to be explained. One does immediately think of both animals in the
words of Jesus: "Do not give dogs what is holy, and do not throw your
pearls before pigs, lest they trample them underfoot and turn to attack you" (Matt. 7:6). Clearly in this text dogs and pigs symbolize the
unconverted who are hostile to the gospel.

Thus the point of the proverb may well be to remind us that these
people, analogous to such animals, never truly experienced an inward change of nature. Notwithstanding the cleanup on the outside, they are still dogs and pigs on the inside (i.e., unregenerate).
"In other words, they were always unclean; they only seemed to have
changed. Perseverance, therefore, is the test of authenticity."[8] Had
these so-called dogs and pigs been genuinely transformed on the
inside, it would have been revealed on the outside in terms of their
behavior. That they returned to their vomit and mire simply proves
that they remained dogs and pigs. No one has explained this more
clearly than John Piper. He writes:

> Peter is not teaching that God's elect can lose their salvation.
> He is most definitely teaching that church members can be
> lost, and people who make outward professions of faith and
> even begin to clean up their lives can turn away from Christ
> and be lost. But in verse 22 he explains to us in a proverb that
> we should not be overly surprised at this: dogs characteristi-
> cally return to their vomit; and no matter how clean you make
> a pig on the outside, if it is still a pig, it will return to the mire.
> In other words, those who leave the way of righteousness,

[8] Schreiner, *1, 2 Peter, Jude*, 365.

never to return, simply show that their inner nature had never been changed. This was Peter's way of saying what 1 John 2:19 says, "They went out from us, but they were not of us, for if they had been of us, they would have continued with us; but they went out that it might be plain that they are all not of us." Or as Jesus said, "He who endures to the end will be saved" (Matthew 10:22). Or as Hebrews puts it, "We share in Christ if we hold our first confidence firm to the end" (Hebrews 3:14). Or as Paul says, "I preached to you the gospel which you received, in which you stand, by which you are saved, *if* you hold it fast" (1 Corinthians 15:1, 2). The whole New Testament is agreed: there is no salvation apart from persevering faith. And persevering faith always works itself out in the way of righteousness. Therefore, to abandon the way of righteousness is to exclude oneself from salvation.[9]

Make no mistake—this passage appears to be a problem for the doctrine of eternal security, but it is not insurmountable. It does not overturn the weight of evidence from such texts as John 6:37–44; 8:31–32, 42–47; 10:28–30; 17:9–15, 24; Romans 5:6–11; 8:1, 28–39; 1 Corinthians 1:4–9; 2 Corinthians 1:21–22; 13:5; Ephesians 1:13–14; Philippians 1:6; 1 Thessalonians 5:23–24; 2 Thessalonians 3:1–5; Hebrews 3:14; 7:23–25; 13:5–6, 20–21; 1 Peter 1:3–5; 1 John 2:19; Jude 1 and 24–25. In other words, we must read 2 Peter 2 in the wider context of the whole New Testament and ask: Which view best accounts for all the biblical evidence? Which view best explains those passages that seem to teach a different perspective? Once again, we can conclude that the New Testament teaches the doctrine of the eternal security of the believer.

[9] John Piper, "Better Never to Have Known the Way," sermon, May 30, 1982, http://www.desiringgod.org.

1 JOHN 3:9

John emphasizes in his first epistle the reality and gravity of sin. In 1 John 1:8 he forcefully labels those who say they have no sin as self-deceived and void of the truth. In 1:10 the claim not to have committed sin is tantamount to calling God a liar, and in 2:1 John clearly implies that Christians will sin (although he writes to help them avoid it). How then do we understand the statement in 3:9 that "no one born of God makes a practice of sinning [more literally, "does not do sin"], for God's seed abides in him, and he cannot keep on sinning [more literally, "is not able to sin"] because he has been born of God"? Following are the major interpretative options (excluding the suggestion of some that John simply contradicts himself).

To avoid the difficulty, some have narrowed the definition of sin to notorious crimes or offenses against love (the view of both Augustine and Luther). Others have suggested that John means that a Christian cannot sin, because what constitutes sin in the life of an unbeliever is not regarded as such by God when committed by a believer. However, this is contrary to both John and the rest of the New Testament.

One interpretation draws a distinction between the old nature in the Christian and the new nature. The old nature may continue to sin, but the new cannot. But how do we isolate a *nature* from the individual himself? We may speak of one's "flesh" and "spirit," but it is always the person who sins or does not sin, not merely a nature.

It's been suggested that John, in the heat of controversial circumstances, breaks forth in holy passion and overemphasizes his point. Yet another perspective is that John is speaking about the ideal rather than the present reality. Or again, insofar as all anticipate that sinlessness will be characteristic in the age to come, and since John believed that the age to come had already been inaugurated (2:8), he understandably asserted the sinlessness of Christians. Greek scholar Dan Wallace embraces a version of this perspective:

The immediate context [of 1 John 3:6 and 9] seems to be speaking in terms of a projected eschatological reality. The larger
section of this letter addresses the bright side of the eschaton:
Since Christians are in the last days, their hope of Christ's im-
minent return should produce godly living (2:28–3:10). The author first articulates how such an eschatological hope should
produce holiness (2:28–3:3). Then, without marking that his
discussion is still in the same vein, he gives a proleptic view of
sanctification (3:4–10)—that is, he gives a hyperbolic picture
of believers vs. unbelievers, implying that even though believers are not yet perfect, they are moving in that direction (3:6,
9 need to be interpreted proleptically), while unbelievers are
moving away from the truth (3:10; cf. 2:19). Thus, the author
states in an absolute manner truths that are not yet true, because he is speaking within the context of eschatological hope
(2:28–3:3) and eschatological judgment (2:18–19).[10]

One author stresses 1 John 3:6, where it is stated that the one
who "abides" in Christ does not sin. He contends that this abiding
in Christ is not descriptive of all Christians but is a condition that
only some believers (those in fellowship) fulfill. The degree of a believer's holiness, then, and his ability to sin or not sin are dependent
on whether he abides. When one is abiding in Christ, he cannot sin.
When one does not abide, one does sin. But 3:9 makes clear why a
Christian doesn't practice sin, indeed, is unable to sin, and it has
nothing to do with abiding. It is because he or she is "born of God."

Others say that the sin of which John speaks in 3:9 is deliberate
sin. The Christian, so they say, cannot commit such deliberate sin
in the face of the Lord. Oh, really? A few take John quite literally.
Hence they believe he is teaching perfectionism. They claim that
1 John 3:9 proves that sinlessness is attainable in this life and that
the statements in 1:8, 10, and especially 2:1 are describing the im-

---

[10] Daniel B. Wallace, *Greek Grammar beyond the Basics: An Exegetical Syntax of the New Testament* (Grand Rapids, MI: Zondervan, 1996), 525.

mature believer who although not yet sinless may still become such through diligent activity and love.

None of the foregoing interpretations is satisfactory. I find either of the next two options to be the most likely.

Some argue that the sin that a believer does not and cannot commit is the "sin that leads to death" (1 John 5:16), namely, hatred of believers and denial of Jesus (see chapter 11 for more detail.)

The view adopted by most commentators is that the sin a Christian does not and cannot commit is habitual, persistent, unrepentant sin. John is not concerned so much with the momentary, individual acts of sin as with the overall characteristic tendencies and inclinations of someone's life. John is not taking a snapshot, but a moving picture. His repeated use of the Greek present tense appears to bear this out. He focuses on the habitual character of the activity in view.[11]

John writes, "No one who abides in him keeps on sinning; no one who keeps on sinning has either seen him or known him" (1 John 3:6). Also, the one who keeps on sinning shows that he has neither seen nor known him. John nowhere denies that a Christian commits acts of sin. He does deny, however, that the Christian sins persistently, without repentance, and habitually as a reflection of the characteristic inclination of his soul.

Note that in 3:9a he says the one begotten of God does not *do* sin. Notes Stott, "It is not the isolated act of sin which is envisaged, but the settled habit of it, indicated by the verb *poiein*, to do or to practise, which is used of 'doing' sin in verses 4a, 8 and 9, of 'doing' lawlessness in verse 4b, and of 'doing' righteousness in 2:29; 3:7, 10a."[12]

John says the one begotten of God, rendered literally, "is not able to sin." But "to sin" is not an aorist infinitive but a *present* infinitive. If the infinitive were aorist, John would be contradicting what he

---

[11] Dan Wallace is one of many Greek grammarians who insists we should avoid deriving such theological truths from use of the present tense. See his arguments in *Greek Grammar Beyond the Basics*, 524–25.
[12] John R. W. Stott, *The Letters of John* (Grand Rapids, MI: Eerdmans, 1996), 130–31.

said in 2:1. The present infinitive indicates that he has in mind the inability of the born-again believer to habitually live in sin as if it were the prevailing temper of his soul.

If the Christian does not practice sin, indeed, cannot practice sin, wherein lies this impossibility? That is to say, *how* does a believer avoid the life of persistent sin so characteristic of the nonbeliever? Stott's answer is excellent:

> Wherein lies this "impossibility"? John's answer is given in two phrases in [verse] 9: *because God's seed remains in him* and *because he has been born of God.*... [It is more probable that] *God's seed* is accurately rendered in the RSV text "God's nature," or "the divine seed" (NEB), and that *in him* refers to the child of God. In this way the two parts of verse 9 become exactly parallel, each part consisting of a statement that the Christian does not or cannot sin, to which is added the reason for such an assertion. The implication of both is this: the new birth involves the acquisition of a new nature through the implanting within us of the very seed or lifegiving power of God. Birth of God is a deep, radical, inward transformation. Moreover, the new nature received at the new birth remains. It exerts a strong internal pressure towards holiness. It is the abiding influence of *God's seed* within everyone who is *born of God*, which enables John to affirm without fear of contradiction that *he cannot go on sinning.*... Indeed, if he should continue to sin, it would indicate that he has never been born again.[13]

When those born of God do sin, conviction, grief, brokenness, misery, and discontent, all of which lead to repentance, will occur.

REVELATION 3:5

The promise to those who conquer continues in Revelation 3:5, a passage that has stirred considerable discussion and controversy.

---

[13] Ibid., 131 (emphasis original).

"The one who conquers," said Jesus, "will be clothed thus in white garments, and *I will never blot his name out of the book of life.* I will confess his name before my Father and before his angels. He who has an ear, let him hear what the Spirit says to the churches."

Some are filled with anxiety that perhaps one day they will fail to conquer and thus have their name blotted out of the book of life. Others read it as a glorious promise of security, a solid rock of assurance, a declaration by Jesus himself that their names will *never* be deleted from God's eternal register. Let's begin our study of it by trying to identify the "book" that Jesus mentions. There are at least five possibilities.

Colin Hemer refers to a particular custom in ancient Athens in which the names of condemned criminals were erased from civic registers before their execution. The Greek word translated "to erase" (*exaleiphein*) "was the technical term for such degradation."[14] As insightful as this may be, it is more likely that we should look for a *biblical* background to this imagery.

In the Old Testament the "book of life" (or its equivalents) was a register of the citizens of the theocratic community of Israel. To have one's name written in the book of life implied the privilege of participation in the temporal blessings of the theocracy, while to be blotted out of the book meant exclusion from those blessings. In other words, this book had reference to the rights of citizenship for the Jewish people (cf. Ex. 32:32; Ps. 69:28; Isa. 4:3).

The concept of a book was also used to portray God's all-inclusive decree; i.e., the very days of one's life are ordained and written in God's "book" before one of them occurs (Ps. 139:16). There is also the notion of books of judgment in which are recorded men's deeds. They serve as that by which or from which one shall be judged (Dan. 7:10; Rev. 20:12).

The most vivid usage, however, is the concept of the book as the

---

[14] Colin Hemer, *The Letters to the Seven Churches of Asia in Their Local Setting* (Sheffield, UK: JSOT Press, 1986), 148.

register of those who have been chosen for salvation from eternity past. Temporal blessings aren't in view but participation in the eternal kingdom of God (see Luke 10:20; Phil. 4:3; Heb. 12:23; Rev. 13:8; 17:8). It would appear from these texts that not all are written in this book, but only the elect.

If it is this fifth and final view that Jesus had in mind, and I believe it is, there are three possible interpretations.

First, Jesus may be saying that it is possible for sinning, unrepentant Christians (such as many at Sardis) to fail to overcome and thereby forfeit their place in the book of life. Their names, already inscribed in the book, will be erased, signifying the loss of their salvation.

Second, to have one's name blotted out refers to something other than salvation. In Revelation 3:1 Jesus referred to the people at Sardis as having a name for being alive, i.e., they had a reputation for spiritual vitality. The idea, then, is that such people are saved but will forfeit any hope of an honorable position in God's coming kingdom. They are saved but will experience shame at the last day. It is not the loss of life per se but the loss of a certain *quality* of life—eternal rewards—that otherwise could have been theirs.

Third, several factors lead me to conclude that John does not envision the possibility of a true Christian forfeiting salvation. All the other promises to the conqueror or overcomer are coined in positive terms, with no threat (implied or explicit) of losing a salvation once gained (see 2:7, 11, 17, 26–27; 3:12, 21). Christians can indeed backslide and sin badly, which the rebukes in the seven letters of Revelation 2–3 indicate. Nevertheless, once again the evidence of the reality of true saving faith is perseverance (i.e., "overcoming"; cf. 1 John 2:19).

The promise here is couched in negative terms for an obvious reason: the names of the "overcomers" (i.e., the elect) have been written in the book from eternity past (see Rev. 13:8; 17:8). There is no indication in Scripture, least of all in Revelation, of additional names being inscribed in the book as a reward for faithfulness or perseverance. Rather, *faithfulness and perseverance are the evidence or fruit of having had one's name written in the book.* Those who worship the beast do so precisely because their names were *not* written in the book (13:8; 17:8).

We need to look more closely at Revelation 13:8 and 17:8 to understand what our Lord is saying in 3:5. According to 13:8,

> All who dwell on earth will worship it [the beast], everyone whose name has not been written before the foundation of the world in the book of life of the Lamb who was slain.

Similarly:

> The beast that you saw was, and is not, and is about to rise from the bottomless pit and go to destruction. And the dwellers on earth whose names have not been written in the book of life from the foundation of the world will marvel to see the beast, because it was and is not and is to come. (17:8)

Note carefully that there are only two groups. First are those whose names have *not* been written in the book of life from eternity past. They "worship" and "marvel" at the beast. The second group consists of those whose names have been written in the book of life, which constitutes the reason why they refuse to give their allegiance to the enemy of Christ. Nowhere does it suggest a third group: people whose names had been written in the book but, because they worshiped the beast, failed to conquer and thus have their names blotted out.

In other words, as John Piper explains, "having our name in the book of life from the foundation of the world seems to mean that God will keep you from falling and grant you to persevere in allegiance to God. Being in the book means you *will not* apostatize."[15]

---

[15] John Piper, "Can the Regenerate Be Erased from the Book of Life?," sermon, December 22, 2006, http://www.desiringgod.org (emphasis original).

Or again, being written in the book means that God is committed to guarding your heart so that you *will* conquer the beast by not yielding to the temptation to worship his name or receive his mark.

Having one's name written in the book from eternity past is what guarantees a life that overcomes, a life that perseveres, a faith that conquers. Piper summarizes:

> This fits with Revelation 3:5, "He who overcomes . . . I will not erase his name from the book of life." The triumph *required* in 3:5 is *guaranteed* in 13:8 and 17:8. This is not a contradiction any more than for Paul to say, "Work out your salvation . . . for God is at work in you to will and to do his good pleasure" (Philippians 2:12–13). It is not nonsense to state the condition: if you conquer, God will not erase your name (3:5); *and* to state the assurance: if your name is written, you will conquer (13:8 and 17:8). God's "written-down-ones" really *must* conquer, and really *will* conquer. One side highlights our responsibility; the other highlights God's sovereignty.[16]

Therefore, Jesus's declaration is a promise to the elect that nothing will ever, by any means (he uses a double negative), prevent them from possessing the eternal inheritance to which they have been ordained. In other words, we must take note of what Jesus does not say. He does *not* say that anyone *will* be erased from the book of life. Rather, he says the overcomers will *not* be erased. His word is a promise of security to overcomers, not a threat of insecurity to those who lapse.

When the disciples returned to Jesus, celebrating their victory over the power of the Devil, our Lord responded by alerting them to an even greater, more glorious, indescribably reassuring truth: "Nevertheless, do not rejoice in this, that the spirits are subject to you, but rejoice that your names are written in heaven" (Luke 10:20).

---

[16] Ibid.

What joy! What comfort! What incentive to love him and praise him and serve him. Jesus will *never* blot my name out of the book of life.

CONCLUSION

Many of you still struggle to grasp how the biblical authors could speak in what appear to be conflicting ways about the security of God's children. Well, so do I. Do they, in fact, conflict? I don't believe they do. I maintain for a variety of reasons that the theology of both testaments is unified and that no biblical author contends for any truth that fundamentally contradicts another. That doesn't mean I'm always able to explain such seemingly disparate texts with sufficient clarity that the discomfort we feel altogether disappears. It does mean that the hermeneutical scales of balance weigh heavily in favor of affirming that those whom God has elected and brought to faith in his Son, Jesus Christ, will never fail to finally and fully reach heaven's gates.

Personally, I'm thankful for the struggle. Confidently assured, as I am, of the Bible's fundamental theological consistency, I'm driven back to these texts again and again to dig ever more deeply into their meaning and to cry out to God ever more desperately for the wisdom and understanding to make sense of what the Spirit has inspired. The fact that we cannot always perfectly harmonize certain texts with others is no excuse to give up trying. Neither is it an excuse to lose confidence in the power of God's Word to teach, reprove, correct, and train us in righteousness that we might be competent and equipped for every good work (2 Tim. 3:16–17).

11

CAN A CHRISTIAN COMMIT THE SIN UNTO DEATH?

"If anyone sees his brother committing a sin not leading to death, he shall ask, and God will give him life—to those who commit sins that do not lead to death. There is sin that leads to death; I do not say that one should pray for that" (1 John 5:16). The problems posed by this passage are innumerable, and therefore so are the interpretations placed upon it. Following are the more cogent views and my critical interaction with each.

SIN UNTO DEATH IS APOSTASY

This first interpretation of 1 John 5:16–17 is one proposed by many Arminians who believe a Christian can apostatize from the faith (i.e., fall from grace) and lose salvation. I. Howard Marshall represents this position.

He argues that the "brother" about whom John speaks is a born-again believer, as the usage of the term "brother" in 1 John would appear to demand (see 1 John 2:9, 10, 11; 3:10, 12 [twice], 13, 14, 15, 16, 17; 4:20 [twice], 21; 5:16). The kind of death John has in mind is spiritual, eternal death, even as the life with which it is contrasted is spiritual and eternal.

That sin that leads to death is any that is incompatible with being a child of God. What sins qualify? According to 1 John, says

Marshall, "sin that leads to death is deliberate refusal to believe in Jesus Christ, to follow God's commands, and to love one's brothers. It leads to death because it includes a deliberate refusal to believe in the One who alone can give life, Jesus Christ, the Son of God."[1]

Conversely, sins that do not lead to death "are those which are committed unwittingly and which do not involve rejection of God and his way of salvation. The sinner is overcome by temptation against his will; he still wants to love God and his neighbor, he still believes in Jesus Christ, he still longs to be freed from sin."[2] Marshall makes this distinction between deliberate apostasy ("sin that leads to death") and unwitting transgression ("sin that does not lead to death") on the basis of the Old Testament distinction between unintentional sins, for which atonement was possible, and deliberate sins, for which the Levitical sacrificial system provided no forgiveness (see Lev. 4:2, 13, 22, 27; 5:15, 17–18; Num. 15:27–31; Deut. 17:12).

Christians can commit both types of sin. If someone sees a brother committing sin that does not lead to death, one should pray for him, and God will use the prayer to give him life. However, if someone sees a Christian brother engaged in open refusal to repent and believe, he is on his way to death. John did not require (but neither does he forbid) that anyone pray for him. Consequently, some Christians may in fact apostatize from the faith by committing sin that leads to their eternal death. The doctrine of eternal security is obviously incompatible with this view.

Several comments should be made about this interpretation. First, the text does not say that the brother commits sin that leads to death. John refers to a brother only with regard to sin that is not unto death. Second, if the sin of the Christian brother is not the kind that leads to death, why must we pray that God would give him life? Marshall answers:

---

[1] I. Howard Marshall, *The Epistles of John*, New International Commentary on the New Testament (Grand Rapids, MI: Eerdmans, 1978), 248.
[2] Ibid.

There is always the danger that a person who sins uncon-
sciously or unwittingly may move to the point of sinning deliberately and then of turning his back completely on God and
the way of forgiveness. Because of this danger, it is essential
that Christians pray for one another lest any of their number
cross the line that leads to open and deliberate rejection of the
way of life. No sin is of such a kind as to prevent forgiveness,
provided that we repent of it. We are to pray for our brothers
that they will repent of all sin. When we do this, we have God's
promise that he will hear our prayers.[3]

But John does not say that the brother was about to cross over some
such line. Indeed, he says just the opposite. It was to the brother who
was *not* committing sin unto death whom God promised to give life.

Furthermore, it would be difficult to think of another New Testament author who affirms the doctrine of eternal security with any
greater conviction or frequency than the apostle John (John 6:37–44;
10:11–18, 27–30; 17:1–2, 7–12; 1 John 5:18). Texts we examined in earlier chapters likewise deny what Marshall affirms (Rom. 8:29–39;
1 Cor. 1:4–9; Phil. 1:6; 1 Thess. 5:23–24; 2 Thess. 2:13–15; 2 Tim. 2:19;
1 Pet. 1:5; Jude 24). Finally, why would John not require us to pray
for an apostate? Marshall says it is because "where a person himself
refuses to seek salvation and forgiveness there is not much point in
praying for him."[4] But isn't that a description that applies to everyone who is not a Christian? Are we not to pray for unbelievers at all?

Raymond Brown, a Roman Catholic scholar, seems to argue for a
position similar to Marshall's. Those who sin unto death, he says, are

former brothers and sisters who have opted to be children of
the devil by going out to the world that prefers darkness to
light. Since Jesus refused to pray for such a world (John 17:9),
the author's adherents should not pray for those who belong

---

[3] Ibid., 248–49.
[4] Ibid., 249.

to the world (1 John 4:5). When his readers came to faith and joined the Johannine community of "brothers," they passed from death to life (1 John 3:14). By leaving the Community the secessionists have shown that they hate the "brothers" and have reversed the process by passing from life to death. In that sense theirs is a sin unto death.[5]

But then in a footnote Brown balks, saying that it is unclear "whether the author would admit they ever had life, since he says that the secessionists never really belonged to the Community (1 John 2:19)."[6] Stephen Smalley also argues for a position in many ways identical to Marshall's. Whereas John "expected his readers to walk in the light as sons of God . . . he did not ignore the possibility that some believing but heretically inclined members of his community might become apostate. . . . We conclude that John attributes the possibility of 'sin which does not lead to death' to believers, but 'mortal sin' to unbelievers who are, *or believers who have become, antichristian*."[7]

BLASPHEMY AGAINST THE HOLY SPIRIT

Others say the sin unto death is blasphemy against the Holy Spirit. This view finds its most able proponent in John Stott.

Stott argues that the brother about whom John speaks in 1 John 5:16–17 is not a Christian man. The term "brother" is being used in "the broader sense of a 'neighbor' or of a nominal Christian, a church member who professes to be a 'brother'" but who in reality is a counterfeit.[8] He appeals to 1 John 2:9–11 as an example of this broad use of the term. Also, how can a Christian with eternal life (1 John 3:14) be given life as John affirms? "How can you give life to

[5] Raymond E. Brown, *The Epistles of John*, Anchor Bible (Garden City, NY: Doubleday, 1982), 636.
[6] Ibid., 636n17.
[7] Stephen S. Smalley, *1, 2, 3 John*, Word Biblical Commentary (Waco, TX: Word, 1984), 299 (emphasis added).
[8] John R. W. Stott, *The Epistles of John: An Introduction and Commentary* (Grand Rapids, MI: Eerdmans, 1976), 190.

one who is already alive? This man is not a Christian, for Christians do not fall into death when they fall into sin."[9] Stott agrees with Marshall that both the life and the death of which John speaks are spiritual and eternal in nature.

However, neither individual in 1 John 5:16 is a Christian. The individual in verse 16b, who commits sin that leads to death, is no more a believer than the brother of verse 16a. He is, most likely, one of the false teachers about whom John has been warning his readers, a counterfeit Christian exposed by his eventual departure from the church (1 John 2:19). The sin that leads to death is the blasphemy of the Holy Spirit (Matt. 12:22–32), that is to say, deliberate and persistent rejection of Jesus Christ. Sin that leads to death, therefore, is not some solitary sin but a settled state of sin. It is the obstinate repudiation of the claims of Christ as made known in the gospel. Although John did not forbid us to pray for someone who blasphemes the Holy Spirit, he did not recommend it because he could not be certain that God would answer it.

First, although it is possible, I think it highly unlikely that John would here refer to a non-Christian as a "brother." Most commentators agree on this point. Second, if both men in verse 16 are nonbelievers, men who reject and disbelieve the gospel of Jesus Christ, how are we to know which one has committed sin that does not lead to death and which one has committed sin that *does* lead to death? How are we supposed to differentiate between an unbeliever and a so-called hardened unbeliever in order that we might pray for the former but not the latter? If John was giving us guidance for knowing when and when not to pray, he was uncharacteristically fuzzy about it.

Third, Stott's view contains a problem that plagues every interpretation, which is context. When we read verse 16 in the light of its preceding context (vv. 14–15), one gets the impression that John was

---

[9] Ibid., 189.

describing a particular kind of prayer that will always be answered. In other words, prayer for a brother whose sin is not unto death is always according to God's will. Consequently, John assures us that in response to such prayer God will give life to the errant brother. If that is correct, the implications are astounding, for it would mean that any non-Christian for whom we pray, assuming that he has not sinned unto death, will be given eternal life. Even were we to interpret "brother" as referring to a Christian, the problem remains. In the latter case, it would imply that any sinning Christian for whom we pray will be restored and renewed. This, however, ascribes more to the power of prayer than the rest of Scripture allows. And although it is not a final authority, experience itself teaches us that not every believer for whom we intercede responds and repents.

Also, what about the man who commits sin that leads to death? In Stott's view, John was saying that he does not recommend we pray for him because it is doubtful if that prayer will be answered. If "sin that leads to death" is blasphemy of the Holy Spirit, as Stott argues, then whoever commits this sin will never be saved. But if it is never God's will to give life to a man who commits sin unto death, why doesn't John explicitly forbid prayer for him? The fact is, John does not require that we pray for such a man, but neither does he prohibit it. But why doesn't he forbid it if by definition (Stott's view) the sin he has committed is unforgivable?

Donald Burdick, although not agreeing in every particular with Stott (Burdick says the "brother" is a believer), suggests that one reason why God may not answer prayer for the man sinning unto death is that "the stubborn will of the sinner may not bend. God," says Burdick, "though sovereign, chooses not to coerce the will and thus violate the integrity of the personality he created in his own image."[10]

But God's effectual grace in converting the sinner is persuasive,

---

[10] Donald W. Burdick, *The Letters of John the Apostle: An In-Depth Commentary* (Chicago: Moody, 1985), 408.

not coercive. More important still, if Burdick's point is valid, why would it not also apply to the brother who commits sin not unto death? Why should we think that God's activity with regard to the brother not sinning unto death is any less coercive or any less a violation of the integrity of his personality than God's activity with regard to the man whose sin *is* unto death? Sin is a stubborn, rebellious act of one's will, both in the believer and the unbeliever, regardless of who commits it. The alleged coercion or violation that concerns Burdick, irrespective of its degree or intensity, is coercion and violation nonetheless.

Perhaps a way to avoid this problem is to understand John to be saying that giving life to brothers who do not sin unto death is something that God often desires to do. Therefore, we should pray to that end. There is no guarantee that it is always God's will to answer such prayers, even though the language of verse 16a is seemingly unconditional. But even this does not explain why John does not forbid prayer for those who, by definition (Stott's view), can never be forgiven of their sins.

Finally, if the man who commits sin unto death is a non-Christian, he is already dead. What, then, could John have meant by saying that if he sins deliberately and persistently, that is, if he blasphemes the Holy Spirit, he will *die*? Stott agrees that the man is already dead, but by persisting in unbelief he will die the "second death" (Rev. 20:11–15). "Spiritually dead already, he will die eternally."[11]

SINS WITHIN AND SINS WITHOUT

The third view is difficult to label. It is somewhat of a mediating position between the views of Marshall and Stott. David M. Scholer is its most convincing defender. Scholer agrees with Marshall that the "brother" is a Christian man and that "death" is spiritual and eternal in nature. He also agrees with Marshall that "sin that leads

---

[11] Stott, *Epistles of John*, 190.

to death" must be identified and defined from within the epistle of
1 John itself. It consists primarily of hating the brothers and denying
that Jesus is the Christ.

However, unlike Marshall he insists that believers do not commit sin that leads to death. Nowhere in the passage, Scholer strenu-
ously claims, is it ever said that a true believer, a "brother," commits
sin that leads to death. Believers do commit sin that does not lead to
death (1 John 1:8; 2:1), and the Christian community is to intercede
for them. Prayer for such sinning Christians will be used by God to
reconfirm the life they already have in Christ (1 John 3:14).

John is concerned not primarily with the sins of unbelievers.
"Prayer," says Scholer, "is not absolutely forbidden concerning the
matter, nor is it said that one who commits the 'sin unto death' is
forever beyond the hope of becoming a member of the believing
community. But throughout 1 John there is a radical separation between the believing community and the unbelieving world so that
prayer for the unbelieving world would not be a 'normal' or 'effec-
tive' practice."[12] Scholer interprets 1 John 3:6, 9 and 5:18 in the light
of 5:16–17. Simply put, the sin that Christians cannot commit is not
a reference to the practice of sin in general or persistence in sin.
Rather, the sin the believer can't commit is "sin that leads to death,"
namely, hatred of believers and denial of Jesus.

Essential to this view is a rephrasing of the closing statement in
verse 16, which reads "I do not say that one should pray for that."
Similarly, the New International Version renders, "I am not saying
that he should pray about that." Both translations make it appear
that John was recommending we not pray about the sin unto death
or for the one who commits it. Scholer would translate this phrase
in another way: "I am not speaking concerning that (i.e., sin unto
death), in order that you should pray." In other words, John's purpose is not to enlist prayer for those who commit sin unto death,

[12] David Scholer, "Sins Within and Sins Without: An Interpretation of 1 John 5:16–18," in *Current Issues in Biblical and Patristic Interpretation*, ed. Gerald Hawthorne (Grand Rapids, MI: Eerdmans, 1975), 243.

although in another context and time it may be legitimate to do so. Rather, it is the sin of believers, sin that is not unto death, that he is speaking about and for which he asks that his readers pray.

To sum up, "sin that leads to death" consists principally of hating believers (what John called "murder") and not confessing Jesus (what John called "lying"). This sin cannot be committed by believers for the simple reason that, by definition, it is the sin that makes one an unbeliever. Believers are guilty of sin that does not lead to death, that is, "they do break fellowship with God (1:6–2:1), but without participating in hating the brothers or denying Jesus."[13] Sin unto death is a sin of those who are "disruptive, heretical outsiders."[14] Consequently, John is not here concerned with them or their sin. His concern is with the sin of insiders, that is, believers within the community of faith.

This view has much to commend it. First, it looks for the meaning of sin that leads to death within 1 John itself and interprets "brother" and "death" in keeping with their usage in this epistle. Second, this view has the advantage of restricting sin unto death to unbelievers. Similar to Stott's interpretation, the "death" into which the sin of these unbelievers leads them is the second, eternal death. Third, Scholer's interpretation supplies us with a cogent solution to other problem texts in 1 John, namely, those that assert that the one born of God cannot or is not able to sin. When 1 John 5:18 (literally, "no one who is born of God sins") is read in the light of 5:16–17, one can see the sense in taking verse 18 to mean, "No one who is born of God sins sin that leads to death."

The only problem one might have with this view is the phrase "God will give him life." To say that this means "he will renew and reconfirm the life he already has" lacks explicit parallel in 1 John and is not, so far as I can tell, stated in precisely these terms elsewhere in

---

[13] Ibid., 242.
[14] Ibid.

the New Testament. But given the number of difficulties the other interpretations face, this one problem is slight by comparison.[15]

PHYSICAL DEATH

The interpretation of Benjamin B. Warfield is one deserving of careful attention. Warfield agrees with Marshall on two points. The "brother" is a Christian, and it is possible for him to commit "sin that leads to death." Warfield disagrees with Marshall in that he affirms eternal security and in his belief that *the death in view is physical, not spiritual*. As we noted earlier, the New Testament does refer to believers suffering illness and occasionally physical death because of persistent and unrepentant sin (see Acts 5:1–11; 1 Cor. 5:5(?); 11:29–30; James 5:14–15, 19–20).

According to Warfield's interpretation, this brother is not sinning in such a way that his physical life is in jeopardy, and since he is a Christian, he already has spiritual life. What, then, could John have meant when he said that God would give him "life" in response to our prayers? Warfield writes:

> We may suppose that by giving life there is meant rather the maintaining or perfecting than the initiating of life. He who lives below his privileges, in whom the life which he has received is languid or weak in its manifestations, is made by our prayers the recipient of fresh vital impulses, or powers, that he may live as the Christian should live. Hitherto living on a plane which can be spoken of only as sinful—though not mortally sinful—he will through our prayers receive newness of life.[16]

In saying that some sin leads to death and other sin does not, John is

---

[15] A helpful discussion of this passage that takes a view quite similar to that of Scholer is found in Robert W. Yarbrough, *1–3 John*, Baker Exegetical Commentary on the New Testament (Grand Rapids, MI: Baker Academic, 2008), 305–14. According to Yarbrough, "sin unto death" refers to "doctrinal convictions, ethical patterns, and relational tendencies—or any combination of these three—which belie one's claim to know the God of light (1:5)" (p. 310). Thus "sin unto death" is "simply violation of the fundamental terms of relationship with God that Jesus Christ mediates" (p. 310).

[16] Benjamin B. Warfield, "Praying for the Erring," *Expository Times* 30 (Summer 1919), 537.

not giving us a criterion by which we may examine the lives of other believers in order to determine whether we should pray for them. He differentiates between these two kinds of sin simply to tell us why it is that some of our prayers are answered and others are not. Warfield explains:

> He is merely saying that of those whom we observe to be sinning in the community, some are, in point of fact, sinning to death, and others not; and that, in point of fact, our prayers will be of benefit to the one and not to the other. Who they are who are sinning to death, we do not in any case know. John does not suppose us to know. Only, in urging us to pray for our sinful brethren, and promising us an answer to our prayers, the gift of life to them, he warns us that there are some for whom our petitions will not thus avail. But he warns us of this, not that we may avoid praying for these unhappy ones, but that we may be prepared for the failure of our prayers in their case.[17]

That no sinner is to be excluded from our prayers is proved, says Warfield, by noting the difference between two Greek words John uses in verse 16 (the NIV renders both these words by the English term, "pray," whereas the ESV renders the first "ask" and the second "pray"). The word in verse 16a translated "he should pray" (*aiteo*) refers to genuine Christian prayer. But the word in verse 16b (*erotao*), likewise translated "he should pray," does not refer to intercessory prayer. Rather, it denotes the asking of questions, the seeking of information, perhaps for the purpose of debate or discussion. If this understanding of the two words is correct,

> the passage would no longer have even the surface appearance of excluding one kind of sinners from our prayers. . . . It would, on the contrary, expressly require us to pray for all sinners, intimating that though there is a sin to death, that is a matter

---

[17] Ibid., 539.

about which we are not to make anxious inquiry before we
pray, but, leaving it to God, we are for ourselves to pray for all
our brethren whom we observe to be living sinful lives.[18]

The purpose of this passage, therefore, is not to set us upon the
task of determining what the sin unto death is or who may or may
not have committed it. The message of the apostle is that sin is
deadly and that if we would have life, we must avoid it. Let us therefore come to the aid of our brothers by praying for one another. If the
sin of the brother for whom we pray is sin unto death, our prayers
will not be answered. His sin has taken him beyond the point at
which our prayers will restore him. However, that his sin is unto
death is something we cannot know before we pray. On the other
hand, if the sin of the brother for whom we pray is not sufficiently
severe so as to put his physical life in jeopardy, God will answer our
prayer and restore this brother to the fullness of joy and spiritual
energy in his daily life with Christ.

Although Warfield's interpretation is intriguing, like the others it is subject to several objections. In the first place, it is unlikely
that "death" means physical death as God's chastisement of an errant believer. Scholer reminds us that in 1 John "death is the state
in which one is before he becomes a believer and out of which he is
transferred unto life (3:14; see John 5:24). The one who does not love
the brothers (that is, believers) remains in death (3:14). Those who
do not love (unbelievers; see 3:9–10; 4:7–8) are not of God (3:10), are
in darkness (2:11; see 1:5) and do not know God (4:8; see 4:7). Thus
it is clear that a 'sin unto death' is one which signifies the complete
absence of any fellowship with God."[19] Of course, this is not to say
that it was impossible for John to shift his emphasis from spiritual
to physical death, but only that it seems improbable.

Second, Warfield agrees that John did not mean to tell us that we

[18] Ibid.
[19] Scholer, "Sins Within and Sins Without," 240.

can actually know whether a brother's sin is unto death. We are to pray, and if his sin is not unto death, God will answer our prayer. If it is unto death, our prayer will fail. But this seems overly subtle of John, if not downright obscure. A straightforward reading of verse 16 appears to indicate that we are to pray for the brother *whom we see* sinning the sort of sin that is not to death. If John did not expect us to be able to know whether his sin was unto death, he surely chose an odd way of saying so.

Finally, there is some doubt as to the validity of drawing a sharp distinction between the Greek words *aiteo* (used in v. 16a) and *erotao* (used in v. 16b). There are several verses in John's Gospel (John 14:14; 16:19, 23) in which the distinction most likely does apply. In 1 John 5, however, most modern commentators insist that the words are synonymous and that the apostle's shift from one to the other is purely stylistic. Note well, though, that even should one accept the distinction between these two terms as valid, it doesn't necessarily follow that death is physical. It is conceivable that all the views we have examined are compatible with this distinction.

CONCLUSION

I find myself a bit reluctant to conclude anything about this passage. But if push comes to shove, and I suspect many of you are waiting for my answer, I would have to endorse the view of Scholer and Yarbrough (among others who advocate this position). A Christian cannot commit the sin unto death because such a sin is precisely what identifies and defines a non-Christian. In any case, this text will probably persist in its (in)famous claim to be one of the most perplexing in all the New Testament until Christ returns and sets us all straight. In the meantime, hermeneutical humility is the wise course to pursue.

CONCLUSION

"Will you be a believer tomorrow morning?" Yes, I too jumped a bit when I first read John Piper's question. Perhaps "jumped" isn't the right word. My reaction was more a combination of cautious trembling together with a presumptuous, "Of course I will! What a silly thing to ask." But I know John Piper had something profoundly important in mind when he posed the question to his readers.[1]

As we've seen, some Christians answer by saying, "Yes, of course I'll be a believer. After all, *once* saved, *always* saved." More than a few, but by no means all, who take this approach insist on their eternal security irrespective of whether they persevere in faith in Jesus Christ. Some even argue that regardless of whether we or anyone else wakes up as a believer tomorrow morning is largely irrelevant to whether we will spend eternity with Christ. The only thing that matters is that at some point in the past we believed the truth of the gospel. The decisive issue isn't whether we persevere in faith but whether we ever believed at all. If we did, we're in. If we didn't, we're out.

Others insist that there's simply no guarantee that anyone will wake up a believer tomorrow morning. Most will, but some likely won't. Before tomorrow, they will have crossed a line of no return. They will have sinned so grievously as to cut themselves off from the saving grace of God. They will have turned their back on Jesus

---

[1] John Piper, "Will You Be a Believer Tomorrow Morning?," sermon, August 20, 2013, http://www.desiring god.org.

Christ and abandoned their faith. Thus when they wake up tomorrow morning they will discover (although by this time they won't care) that God likewise has abandoned them.

The position taken in this book (and by John Piper in his blog post) is that those who genuinely believed at some point in the past (whether days or decades ago) will most assuredly wake up still believers tomorrow morning. That doesn't mean they will remain secure in their salvation simply because of that past belief. It means they are secure because the God in whom they put their trust preserves them in that faith, apart from which there is no hope or eternal life.

Piper unpacks this by focusing on three truths that we've touched on repeatedly in this book.

First, we must persevere in faith to enter heaven (see Mark 13:13; 1 Cor. 15:1–2; 2 Tim. 2:12). Not to persevere is to perish. The Arminian is closer to the truth on this point than the antinomian.

Second, God will preserve us in our faith even though at times we may doubt and wander away from the path of righteousness. But he will always remain true to his promise by ensuring that none of his children will fall so far as to finally and forever fail. "Enduring in faith," says Piper, "is not owing to our first profession of faith the way health is owing to a one-time vaccination. Enduring faith happens because the great physician does his sustaining work every day. We keep believing in Christ not because of antibodies left over from conversion, but because God does his life-giving, faith-preserving work every day." This is something we saw in our study of such passages as 1 Corinthians 1:8–9; Philippians 1:6; and Jude 24 (see also Jer. 32:40).

The third and most reassuring truth is that because God will preserve us, we will in fact persevere. We will endure in faith. We know this to be true, among other reasons and on the basis of other texts, because "those whom he foreknew he also predestined to be conformed to the image of his Son, in order that he might be the firstborn among many brothers. And those whom he predestined he also called, and those whom he called he also justified, and those whom he justified he also glorified" (Rom. 8:29–30).

Romans 8 and numerous similar texts account for why the perseverance of the saints is ultimately more about God and his character than it is about you and yours. That's not to say your character doesn't count. We mustn't forget that without holiness "no one will see the Lord" (Heb. 12:14b; see also Matt. 5:8). But without the Lord, no one will see holiness. Our obedient faith, both today and tomorrow morning, is the fruit of God's faithfulness to preserve us to the end. And to the end we must (and will) persevere.

All biblical truth is reason to rejoice, but perhaps none more so than this one. What encouragement! What joy! What strength for today's problems! What peace for tomorrow's threats! God has said it. God will do it. He will never leave us or by any means forsake us (see Heb. 13:5), which means he will do whatever is necessary to guarantee that we will never leave him or forsake his Son.

And what about Charley (or Charlene)? That question remains a difficult and often painful one, as Charley may well be someone we know and love and in whose spiritual welfare we have invested considerable time and on whose behalf we have shed countless tears. We all undoubtedly want to believe that a Charley or a Charlene is genuinely born again, a justified and adopted child of God who, for whatever reason, has temporarily lapsed into unrepentant sin. We all desperately want to believe that in time God's loving discipline and faithfulness to his saving promise will restore him or her to a vibrant and Christ-exalting lifestyle. But we must also acknowledge that Scripture does not give us warrant for assuring them that no matter what has happened "it is" still "well" with their soul. Sadly, it may not be.

In the final analysis, as much as we'd like to have a well-grounded reason to draw a definitive conclusion about his or her salvation, only "the Lord knows those who are his" (2 Tim. 2:19a). We don't.

General Index

Simon, 52–53
sin, of blasphemy of the Holy
    Spirit, 32–33, 35, 178–81; and
    brokenness, 39, 42; continuing
    in, 157–58, 165–67; conviction
    of, 28, 38, 97; unto death, 175–
    87; and restoration, 160–61;
    unforgivable, 34–40; uninten-
    tional vs. deliberate, 176–77; of
    unrepentance, 25, 98, 152
spiritual self-control, 140
Stott, John, 137, 167–68, 178–82
suffering, 126

tribulation, 83

unbelief, 30–31, 36
unregenerate, 48, 110–15

Wallace, Dan, 165–66
Warfield, Benjamin, 184–86
weakness, 24
Weeks, Noel, 158
works, 30, 46, 145–50

Yarbrough, Robert, 184n, 187

SCRIPTURE INDEX

Also Available from Sam Storms

More Precious Than GOLD   STORMS   CROSSWAY

a Sincere *and* Pure Devotion *to* Christ   VOLUME I   STORMS   :: CROSSWAY

a Sincere *and* Pure Devotion *to* Christ   VOLUME II   STORMS   :: CROSSWAY

SIGNS *of the* SPIRIT   STORMS   CROSSWAY

the HOPE *of* Glory   STORMS

Tough Topics   Sam Storms

CHOSEN *for* LIFE   STORMS   CROSSWAY